Knitting Simple Sweaters from Luxurious Yarns

Knitting Simple Sweaters from Luxurious Yarns

Marilyn Saitz Cohen

LARK BOOKS

A Division of Sterling Publishing Co., Inc.
New York

Editor: MARCIANNE MILLER
Art Director: DANA M. IRWIN
Photographer: SANDRA STAMBAUGH
Cover Designer: BARBARA ZARETSKY
Assistant Art Director: HANNES CHAREN
Illustrator: ORRIN LUNDGREN
Assistant Editor: NATHALIE MORNU
Production Assistance: SHANNON YOKELEY
Editorial Assistance: DELORES GOSNELL, VERONIKA ALICE GUNTER,
ANNE HOLLYFIELD, RAIN NEWCOMB
Makeup and Hair: FRANCELLE D
Assistant Photographer and Lighting Design: SEAN MOSER

The Library of Congress has cataloged the hardcover edition as follows:

Cohen, Marilyn Saitz.
    Knitting simple sweaters from luxurious yarns / Marilyn Saitz Cohen.
        p. cm.
    ISBN 1-57990-423-8
    1. Knitting--Patterns. 2. Sweaters. I. Title
    TT825.C635 2003
    746.43'20432--DC21

                                                    2003004392

10 9 8 7 6 5 4 3 2 1

Published by Lark Books, a division of
Sterling Publishing Co., Inc.
387 Park Avenue South, New York, N.Y. 10016

First Paperback Edition 2006
© 2003, Marilyn Saitz Cohen

Distributed in Canada by Sterling Publishing,
c/o Canadian Manda Group, 165 Dufferin Street
Toronto, Ontario, Canada M6K 3H6

Distributed in the U.K. by Guild of Master Craftsman Publications Ltd.,
Castle Place, 166 High Street, Lewes, East Sussex, England BN7 1XU
Tel: (+ 44) 1273 477374, Fax: (+ 44) 1273 478606,
Email: pubs@thegmcgroup.com, Web: www.gmcpublications.com

Distributed in Australia by Capricorn Link (Australia) Pty Ltd.,
P.O. Box 704, Windsor, NSW 2756 Australia

If you have questions or comments about this book, please contact:
Lark Books, 67 Broadway, Asheville, NC 28801
(828) 253-0467

Manufactured in China

ISBN 13: 978-1-57990-744-0
ISBN 10: 1-57990-423-8 (hardcover) 1-57990-744-X (paperback)

For information about custom editions, special sales, premium and corporate
purchases, please contact Sterling Special Sales Department at 800-805-5489
or specialsales@sterlingpub.com.

With my love always, to my husband, Bo,
and my daughter, Lisa

Table of Contents

Introduction	8
About the Projects	14
Silk & Mohair Tweed Crew Neck	16
Pearly-Shine Sleeveless	20
Versatile Ballet-Neck	24
Dramatic Scoop Neck	28
Grey Angora Boatneck	32
Sleeveless Black Magic	36
Chocolate Decadence	40
Pale Aqua Turtleneck	44
Powder Blue Boatneck	48
Vibrant Red Mohair	52
Comfy Winter Turtleneck	56
Cozy Funnel Neck	60
Silvery Sweater	66
Regal Funnel Neck	70
Exquisite Lattice Cables	74
Finest Cotton Eyelet Rib	75
Quintessential Cardigan	80
Café Au Lait Sleeveless	84
Sequined Mohair	87
Pashmina Cashmere Hooded Sweater	90
Perfect Turtleneck	94
Glittery Bronze Tank Top	98
Serene Green with One Cable	102
Look of Linen	106
Lilacs & Lace Eyelet Rib	110
La Dolce Vita Silky Ribbon Knit	114
Bamboo Stitch V-Neck	118
Lacy & Light Mohair	122
Acknowledgments	126
Index	128

L Like most women, I love feeling stylish and comfortable at the same time, so unique and luxurious sweaters have always been the mainstay of my wardrobe. About 20 years ago, after searching unsuccessfully in boutiques and department stores for the styles, fit, and colors that I wanted, I revived the knitting skills I had learned as a child and began to teach myself how to design sweaters.

H Haunting the local yarn shops became my obsession, every inch of the displays of yarn was a veritable feast for my senses. At first the velvety chenilles and thick, fluffy mohairs intrigued me and I knit many sweaters from these yarns, following simple patterns. Soon, other yarns beckoned—silks, cottons, angoras, rayon blends, and ribbons. Each new sweater project became a lesson in the ways of knitting with luxury yarns. I began to understand how styles were developed, and how to modify and change patterns so that the style would be compatible with the yarn and the fit would be as close to perfect as possible.

One day I became brave enough to wear one of my designs while shopping at a local boutique.

The owner admired the sweater and asked "Where did you buy it?" I laughed, "I knit it myself." Then she asked if she could order half a dozen in various colors and have them delivered in four weeks!

I felt compelled to say yes, even though I had no idea how I would ever be able to do it. I found yarn in six colors and enlisted the help of my mother and mother-in-law. We all knit furiously— and to our amazement we got the sweaters in on time. The sweaters sold quickly and when the reorder call came in, we were all thrilled. That was the beginning of a design career that grew into a cottage industry, using the skills of a dozen, and at times more, fine local knitters who lived nearby in Marin County, California.

The Art of
KNITTING WITH LUXURY YARNS

A handknit sweater is a very special work of art. As an artist, I approach a knitting project with the same creative questions I bring to my drawing board, just as you, too, contemplate the creation of any new artistic expression. What are the colors, shapes, textures, and forms that you need to consider? What feelings to evoke? Should the visuals be subdued or exciting? Which tools should you use? Instead of the artist's brushes, pens, inks, and paints, the knitter's tools are needles and luxurious yarns—cashmeres, silks, merino wools, mercerized cottons, kid mohairs, angoras, microfibers, and rayons.

Design principles for sweaters follow the same inspiration as other forms of art. During the design phase of a sweater, you choose from a myriad of colors, stitch patterns, and yarn textures. You seek out styles that are simple and elegant, easy to knit, comfortable to wear, timeless yet contemporary— the kinds of sweaters in this book. Wanting to share the joy of knitting with luxury yarns with as many other knitters as possible, I chose designs that are easy to knit—whether you're a beginner, expert, or somewhere in-between, you'll find designs that are suitable for your experience.

Knitting with luxury yarns is an exercise in being inspired. Their beauty will never cease to amaze you; you'll never tire of feeling their textures beneath your fingers as you work. In their "waiting-to-be-knit" form, these yarns are already stunning and easily adaptable to simple designs. When knit, they make the simplest sweater design look elegant and sophisticated. And when worn, a sweater made of luxury yarns feels special because of its superior quality and the way in which it shows off its color and texture.

Techniques for
KNITTING WITH LUXURY YARNS

Knitting with luxury yarns is not unlike knitting with everyday yarns. With both, you have the same concerns of color choices, style, pattern, stitch, and gauge determination. However, working with these yarns requires some additional consideration.

CHECK YOUR GAUGE

It's essential to make a large swatch to accurately determine the gauge before beginning any knitting project. Each knitter has her or his own way of holding the needles and the yarn, so even one-quarter of a stitch per inch difference from the suggested gauge and needle size in a chosen sweater design will alter the measurements and final fit. I have emphasized this point in each set of instructions by repeating "Always take time to check your gauge."

If your swatch doesn't measure the same as my gauge, then choose the next needle size, larger or smaller, make another swatch, and remeasure until your test matches the suggested gauge. Only then can you be sure that the final measurements will be correct.

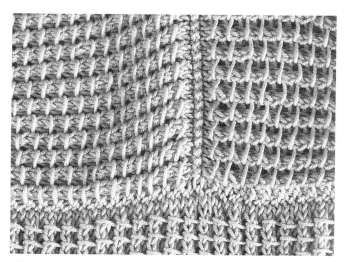

All the sweater designs call for a shoulder seam done in whipstitch.

SPECIAL FINISHING: THE SHOULDER SEAM

Special finishing of the shoulder seam is an integral part of my designs. Side and sleeve seams are unobtrusive, but shoulder seams show prominently. That's why using a whipstitch seam gives a uniquely tailored and pretty finish. Here's how to do it: with right sides facing, sew down through the inner edge of the back bound-off stitch and up through the inner edge of the front bound-off stitch.

MAKING AN EASY, ENDURING FIT

The most demanding facet of sweater designing is the fit. What sweater lovers strive for most consistently are easy-fitting, enduring styles. Notice that many of the sweaters in this book were designed with "dropped shoulders." This means that there is no armhole shaping (no increasing or decreasing) and that the fit will be easy, casual, and very comfortable. You'll also notice that the ribbings at sleeve cuffs and bottom edges are kept to a minimum so that the sweater will hang straight on your body for a sleeker and more flattering fit and ease of movement.

Dropped shoulders create a casual fit and timeless style.

Sweaters in single colors are elegant and simple—the best way to show off luxury yarns.

CHOOSING COLOR AND YARN

Luxury yarn choices are delightfully endless. For fall and winter designs, start your search, with some of the best of the classic luxurious yarns: 100 percent cashmere, extra fine merino, merino and cashmere blends, merino and silk mixes, angora combined with silk or wool, 100 percent silk, and kid mohair. The most classic color choices are the neutrals (creamy white, beige, blush, grey, brown), burgundy, an occasional soft green or blue, basic black, and every so often a true red.

For spring and summer, look for the best of the mercerized cottons, linens, and linen blends with cotton or rayon, velvety microfibers, smooth shiny ribbons, nylon or cotton tapes, and light lacy yarns with lots of texture. Enjoy the palest pastels for spring and summer, the beige linens, the stark white and inky black cottons.

A single color best shows off the luxury yarns, so most of the sweaters in the book are single color designs. Light grey, beige, white, cream, pastels, or bright colors highlight texture and pattern beautifully. Dark colors in cold weather or warm—black, burgundy, brown and charcoal—look richly intense when the yarn has its own unique texture, such as a soft, furry mohair, a smooth shiny ribbon, or a bouclé.

CHOOSING THE STITCHES

Luxurious yarns lend themselves to any number of infinite stitches and patterns. The smoothly knit plain stockinette stitch of a fine cashmere sweater rivals the beauty of an intricately cabled one. Cotton or linens knit in a tight rib for a tailored or sporty look can be especially feminine and romantic when worked in an open lace stitch. Shiny bold textures of wide ribbon can be knit into a smoothly elegant long-sleeved evening sweater or a trendy tank top. Smoothest mercerized cotton can be knit into a three-dimensional bobble stitch fantasy or a simple knit and purl combination with a flat silky finish.

About the Projects

In *Knitting Simple Sweaters from Luxurious Yarns* you'll find 28 of my favorite sweater designs. They are based on classic styles and simple lines we all love—the ballet-neck, boatneck, crew neck, funnel neck, turtleneck, and V-neck—those timeless designs that look as current now as they did 20 years ago.

Each project shows the finished bust measurement for small, medium, and large sizes, and the type of yarn and the amount you'll need for each size. All the measurements are given in U.S., followed by metric equivalents in parentheses. Of course, amounts are approximate, so don't worry if the amount of yarn you use differs from the amount indicated. In case you wanted to make the exact sweater in the photo, the specific yarns used for the sweater are listed at the end of the instructions.

Just as you would for any knitting project, read the instructions all the way through before you start. Gather all your yarns and needles for the project in one convenient place so that if your knitting is interrupted, you can easily pick up where you left off.

I am always dazzled by the thousands of luxurious yarns produced by talented yarn designers and manufacturers, all artists themselves. Each ball of yarn seems like a small soft sculpture waiting to become part of a finished work of art—your special handknit sweater. And that is the creative passion on which this book is based. I hope that it will give you many hours of knitting pleasure, and that you enjoy reading this book as much as I enjoyed writing it.

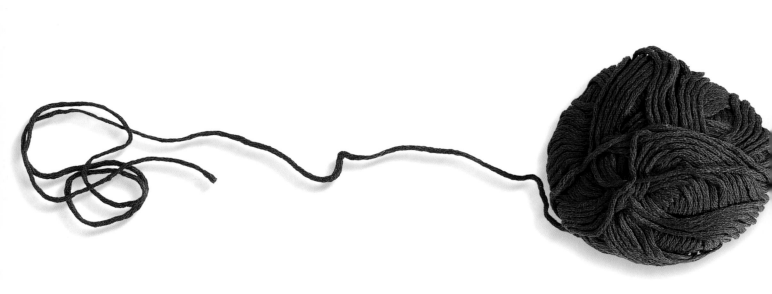

Silk & Mohair
TWEED CREW NECK

IF YOU LOVE TWEEDS, THIS IS THE SWEATER FOR YOU. THE STYLE IS AN EVERLASTING CREW NECK, WARM AND COMFORTABLE, NOT TOO BIG, NOT TOO SMALL, IN A NEUTRAL COLOR COMBINATION TO WEAR SEASON AFTER SEASON. TWO UNUSUAL YARNS, A SUBTLE BEIGE TWEEDY SILK AND A VERY FINE SOFT KID MOHAIR, ARE COMBINED FOR THE BODY AND SLEEVES. TWO STRANDS OF THE BLACK MOHAIR ARE HELD TOGETHER FOR ALL THE RIBBINGS. AN EASY STOCKINETTE IS THE STITCH OF CHOICE ON LARGE NEEDLES FOR THE BODY, SLEEVES, AND RIBBINGS.

Design Tip

Two yarns are held together throughout this project. It would be fun to choose from a variety of yarn textures and colors to combine and create your own personally selected tweed.

Sizes
Small (medium, large)

Finished Measurements
40 (42, 44) inches (101.5, 106.5, 112 cm)

Materials
Approx. 686 (784, 882) yards (627, 717, 806.5 m) of 100% silk yarn, worsted weight
Approx. 924 (1078, 1232) yards (845, 985.5, 1126.5 m) of 70% super kid mohair/25% polyamid/5% wool yarn, sport weight
Knitting needles in size 10 U.S. (6 mm)
Tapestry needle for sewing seams

Gauge
12 sts and 18 rows = 4 inches (10 cm)
Always take time to check your gauge.

Pattern Stitches
Stockinette
Row 1: Knit, right side.
Row 2: Purl, wrong side.

Rib
Row 1: K1, p1. Repeat row 1.

Back
With 2 strands of mohair held together, cast on 60 (64, 68) sts.
K1, p1 rib for 1 inch (2.5 cm).
Continue with 1 strand of mohair and 1 strand of silk held together and work in stockinette to 21 (22, 23) inches (53.5, 55, 58.5 cm).
Bind off.

Front
Work same as back to 18$\frac{1}{2}$ (19$\frac{1}{2}$, 20$\frac{1}{2}$) inches (47, 49.5, 52 cm), ending with a purl row.
To shape neck: k22 (24, 26) sts across; with second balls of yarn (silk and mohair held together), bind off 16 sts, k22 (24, 26). Decrease 1 st each side of neck edge every other row until front measures 21 (22, 23) inches (53.5, 56, 58.5 cm).
Bind off.

Sleeves
With 2 strands of mohair held together, cast on 26 (28, 30) sts.
K1, p1 rib for 2 inches (5 cm).
Continue, with 1 strand of silk and 1 strand of mohair held together, in stockinette, increasing 1 st each side every 6th row to 19 (19$\frac{1}{2}$, 20) inches (48.5, 49.5, 51 cm).
Bind off.

Finishing
Sew one shoulder seam. With 2 strands of mohair, pick up approximately 68 (70, 72) sts around neck and k1, p1 rib for $\frac{3}{4}$ inch (2 cm).
Bind off loosely.
Sew remaining shoulder seam, armhole, side, and sleeve seams.

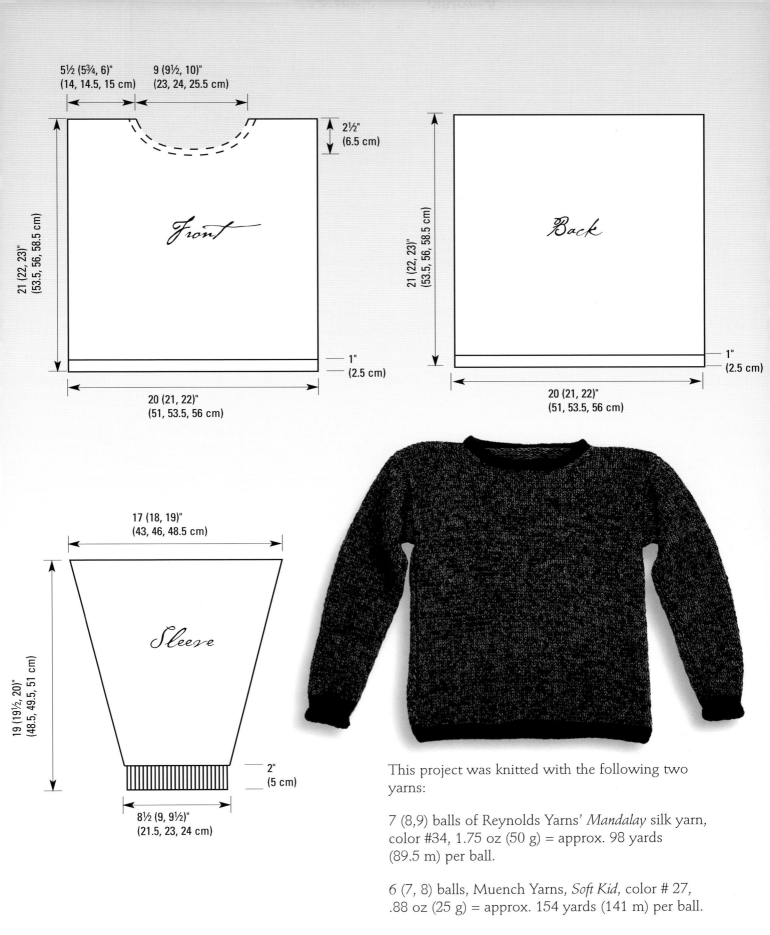

5½ (5¾, 6)"
(14, 14.5, 15 cm)

9 (9½, 10)"
(23, 24, 25.5 cm)

2½"
(6.5 cm)

Front

21 (22, 23)"
(53.5, 56, 58.5 cm)

1"
(2.5 cm)

20 (21, 22)"
(51, 53.5, 56 cm)

Back

21 (22, 23)"
(53.5, 56, 58.5 cm)

1"
(2.5 cm)

20 (21, 22)"
(51, 53.5, 56 cm)

17 (18, 19)"
(43, 46, 48.5 cm)

Sleeve

19 (19½, 20)"
(48.5, 49.5, 51 cm)

2"
(5 cm)

8½ (9, 9½)"
(21.5, 23, 24 cm)

This project was knitted with the following two yarns:

7 (8,9) balls of Reynolds Yarns' *Mandalay* silk yarn, color #34, 1.75 oz (50 g) = approx. 98 yards (89.5 m) per ball.

6 (7, 8) balls, Muench Yarns, *Soft Kid*, color # 27, .88 oz (25 g) = approx. 154 yards (141 m) per ball.

Pearly-Shine
SLEEVELESS

A LITTLE BIT OF VISCOSE AND POLYESTER ADD A SUBTLE PEARLY SHINE TO THIS COTTON SLEEVELESS TURTLENECK. THERE ARE ONLY TWO PIECES TO KNIT—THE FRONT AND THE BACK, AND THEY ARE BOTH THE SAME. PICTURE IT WORN UNDER A TAILORED JACKET ANY TIME OF YEAR. OR LET IT SHINE BY ITSELF IN THE SUMMERTIME, OVER CASUAL JEANS OR SLINKY SILK PANTS.

Design Tip

If you are wondering about the practicality of this type of yarn, have no fear. Even though it's white and sparkly, it's completely hand-washable in cold water. Also, note that there is no finishing needed at the armholes or turtleneck because the material will curl and look perfectly finished when worn.

Sizes
Small (medium, large)

Finished Measurements
34 (36, 38) inches (86.5, 91.5, 96.5 cm)

Materials
Approx. 891 (990, 1089) yards (814.5, 905, 996 m) of 70% cotton/20 % viscose/10% polyester yarn, worsted weight
Knitting needles in size 7 U.S. (4.5 mm)
Tapestry needle for sewing seams

Gauge
20 sts and 26 rows = 4 inches (10 cm)
Always take time to check your gauge.

Pattern Stitches
Stockinette
Row 1: Knit, right side.
Row 2: Purl, wrong side.

Rib
Row 1: Knit 1, purl 1. Repeat row 1.

Back
Cast on 90 (96, 100) sts.
K1, p1 rib for 1/2 inch (1.5 cm).
Work even in stockinette to 12 1/2 (13 1/2, 14 1/2) inches (32, 34.5, 37 cm).
Shape armhole: Bind off 3 sts at beginning of next two rows; then 2 sts at beginning of next 2 rows, then 1 st each side every other row, 6 times.
Work even on 68 (74, 78) sts until armhole measures 7 1/2 (8, 8 1/2) inches (19, 20.5, 21.5 cm) and total measurement is 20 (21, 22) inches (51, 53.5, 56 cm).
Then, bind off 10 sts at beginning of next 2 rows for shoulders and continue on 48 (54, 58) sts for 7 inches (18 cm). Bind off.

Front
Work same as back.

Finishing
Sew seams. Turtleneck will curl forward.

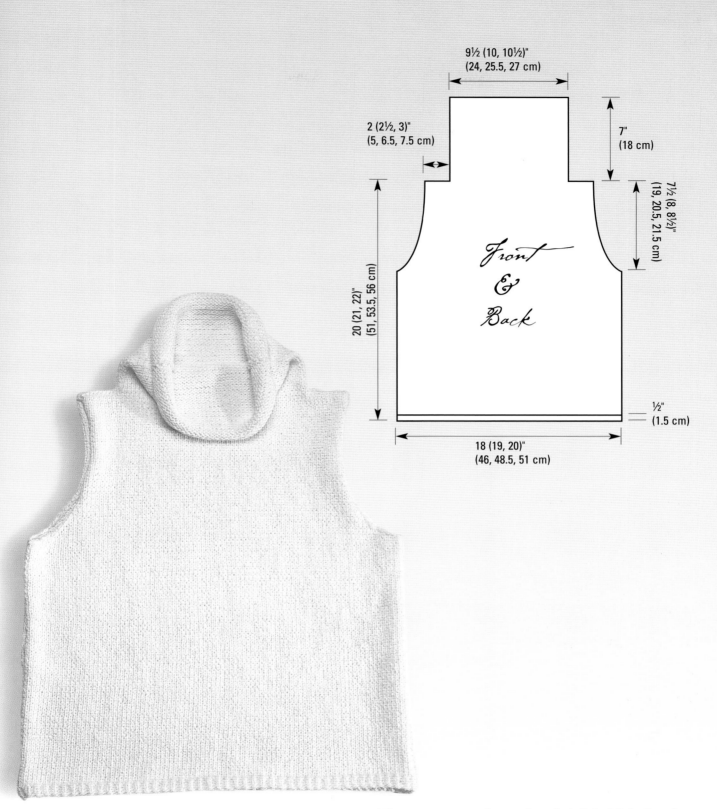

9½ (10, 10½)"
(24, 25.5, 27 cm)

2 (2½, 3)"
(5, 6.5, 7.5 cm)

7"
(18 cm)

7½ (8, 8½)"
(19, 20.5, 21.5 cm)

20 (21, 22)"
(51, 53.5, 56 cm)

Front & Back

½"
(1.5 cm)

18 (19, 20)"
(46, 48.5, 51 cm)

This project was knitted with 9 (10, 11) balls of Muench Yarns' *String of Pearls*, color #3011, 1.75 oz (50 g) = approx. 99 yards (90 m) per ball.

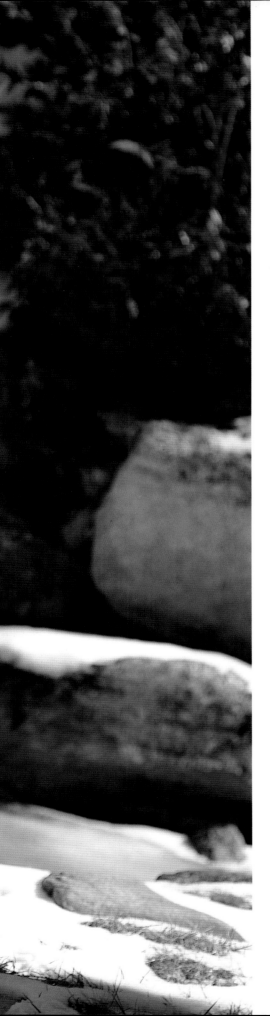

Versatile BALLET-NECK

THE TEMPO IS *ADAGIO*, SLOW TO BEGIN

WITH, IN THIS BALLET-NECK SWEATER, BUT

AS YOU GET USED TO THE PURL 2-KNIT 3

RIB-STITCH RHYTHM, IT SOON BECOMES *ANDANTE*. BY

THE TIME YOUR FINGERS ARE DANCING TOWARDS THE

FINISH, THE MODE IS *ALLEGRETTO*. THIS ONE-SIZE-FITS-

ALL, STRETCHY PULLOVER IN A COTTON-LINEN MIX

WILL TAKE YOU THROUGH ALL THE SEASONS, EVEN WIN-

TER IF WORN OVER A TURTLENECK.

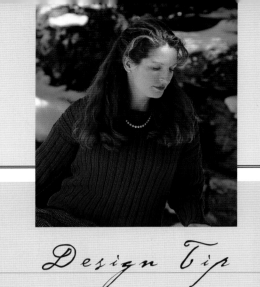

Design Tip

*T*he rib stitch allows for lots of stretch, but will pull back into its shape when off the body. I chose burgundy to emphasize the stitch, but other colors that will also show it off are natural linen, pale rose, soft teal, light turquoise, deep purple, maize, and celadon.

Sizes

One size fits all

Finished Measurements

Stretches from 36 to 48 inches (91.5 to 122 cm)

Materials

Approx. 1144 yards (1046 m) of 50% cotton/50% linen yarn, bulky weight
Knitting needles in size 10 U.S. (6 mm)
Crochet hook size H
Tapestry needle for sewing seams

Gauge

20 sts and 20 rows = 4 inches (10 cm)
Always take time to check your gauge.

Pattern Stitch

Purl 2, knit 3 rib. Multiple of 5 + 2 + 2 edge stitches.
Row 1: (right side): K1 (edge st), *p2, knit 3*. Repeat from * to *, end with p2 and k1 (edge st).
Row 2: P1 (edge st), *k2, p3*. Repeat from * to *, end with k2, p1 (edge st).
Repeat these 2 rows for pattern.

Back

Cast on 99 sts.
Work in pattern to 21 inches (53.5 cm).
Bind off.

Front

Work same as back to 18 inches (46 cm).
Shape neck: on a right side row, work across 38 sts and with 2nd ball of yarn, bind off 23 sts. Work remaining 38 sts. Decrease 1 st each side of neck edge, each row, to 21 inches (53.5 cm).
Bind off.

Sleeves

Cast on 44 sts.
Work in pattern, increasing 1 st each side every 5th row, to 19 inches (48.5 cm).
Bind off.

Finishing

Sew shoulder, armhole, sleeve, and side seams.
With right side facing, using crochet hook H, slip-stitch around neck, going into the front half of every other stitch.

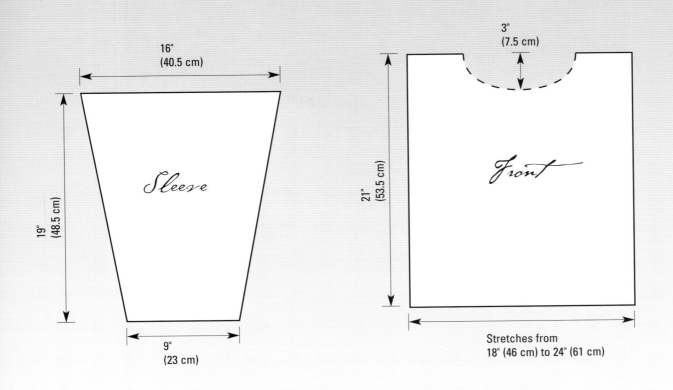

16"
(40.5 cm)

19"
(48.5 cm)

Sleeve

9"
(23 cm)

3"
(7.5 cm)

21"
(53.5 cm)

Front

Stretches from
18" (46 cm) to 24" (61 cm)

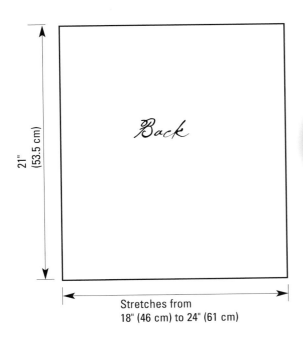

21"
(53.5 cm)

Back

Stretches from
18" (46 cm) to 24" (61 cm)

This project was knitted with 11 balls of Reynolds
Yarns' *Morocco*, color #15, 3.5 oz (100 g) = approx.
104 yards (95 m) per ball.

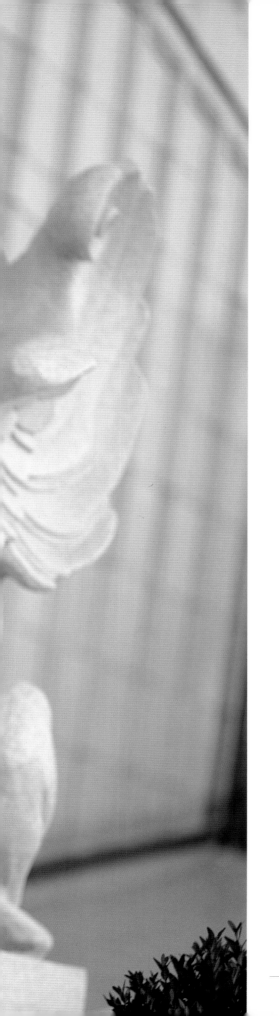

Dramatic SCOOP NECK

SHINY, SOFT, DRAPEY, LIGHT-WEIGHT, AND SEMI-FITTED—THIS BLACK, NECKLINE-FLATTERING SWEATER MIGHT TURN OUT TO BE THE MAINSTAY OF YOUR WARDROBE. THE NYLON RIBBON YARN REQUIRES SMALL NEEDLES AND CARE TAKEN IN THE KNITTING TO AVOID SNAGS, BUT IT'S AN EASY STOCKINETTE STITCH. COMFORTABLE DURING THE DAY, ELEGANT AT NIGHT, IT ALSO FOLDS COMPACTLY FOR TRAVEL.

Sizes
Small (medium, large)

Finished Measurements
36 (38, 40) inches (91.5, 96.5, 101.5 cm)

Materials
Approx.1287 (1430, 1573) yards (1177,1307.5, 1438.5 m) of 100% nylon ribbon yarn, fingering weight
Knitting needles in size 4 U.S. (3.5 mm)
Crochet hook size D
Tapestry needle for sewing seams

Gauge
26 sts and 38 rows = 4 inches (10 cm)
Always take time to check your gauge.

Pattern Stitches
Stockinette
Row 1: Knit, right side.
Row 2: Purl, wrong side.

Rib
Row 1: K1, p1. Repeat row 1.

Back
Cast on 118 (126, 132) sts.
K1, p1 rib for $\frac{1}{2}$ inch (1.5cm).
Work in stockinette to 21 (22, 23) inches (53.5, 56, 58.5 cm). Bind off.

Front
Work same as back to 18 (19, 20) inches (46, 48.5, 51 cm), ending on a wrong side row.
To shape neckline: k 46, and with second ball of yarn bind off 26 (34, 40) sts, k46.
Continue to work both sides at the same time and bind off from each neck edge 3 sts twice, 2 sts twice, then decrease 1 st every other row to 21 (22, 23) inches (53.5, 56, 58.5 cm).
Bind off remaining stitches each side.

Sleeves
Cast on 52 (56, 60) sts.
Work in stockinette, increasing 1 st each side every 7th row, to 18$\frac{1}{2}$ (19$\frac{1}{2}$, 20) inches (47, 49.5, 51 cm). Bind off.

Finishing
Sew shoulder, side, and sleeve seams.
Slip stitch around neckline carefully and evenly with crochet hook D.

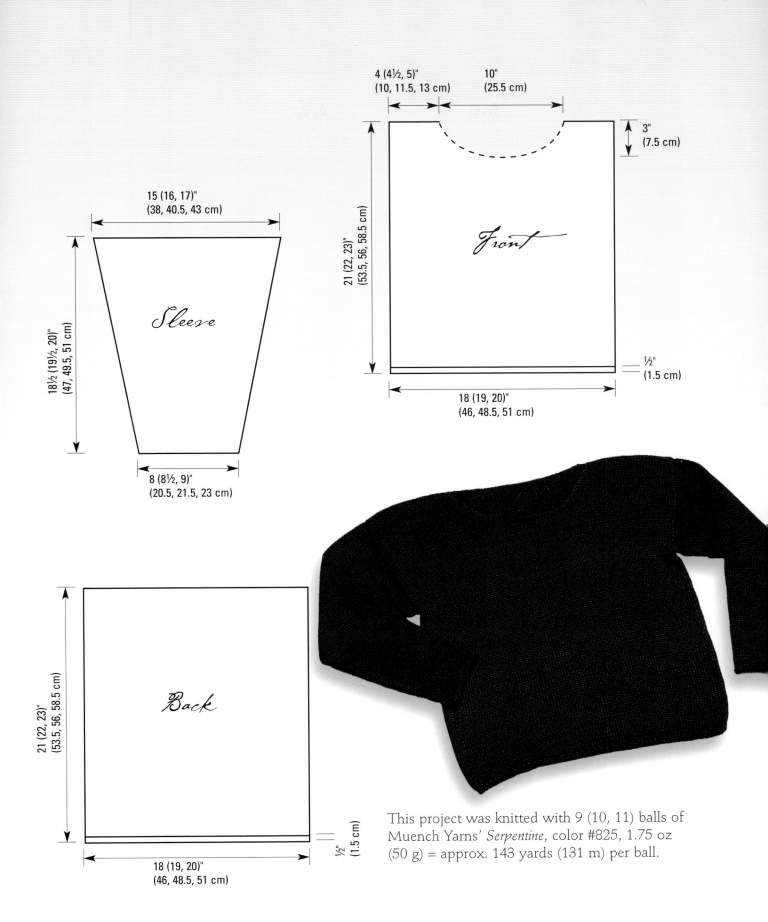

15 (16, 17)"
(38, 40.5, 43 cm)

Sleeve

18½ (19½, 20)"
(47, 49.5, 51 cm)

8 (8½, 9)"
(20.5, 21.5, 23 cm)

4 (4½, 5)"
(10, 11.5, 13 cm)

10"
(25.5 cm)

3"
(7.5 cm)

Front

21 (22, 23)"
(53.5, 56, 58.5 cm)

½"
(1.5 cm)

18 (19, 20)"
(46, 48.5, 51 cm)

21 (22, 23)"
(53.5, 56, 58.5 cm)

Back

½"
(1.5 cm)

18 (19, 20)"
(46, 48.5, 51 cm)

This project was knitted with 9 (10, 11) balls of
Muench Yarns' *Serpentine*, color #825, 1.75 oz
(50 g) = approx. 143 yards (131 m) per ball.

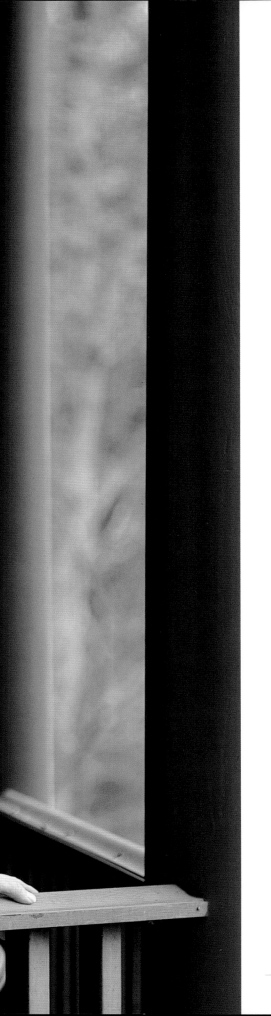

Grey Angora
BOATNECK

Between black and white, there are countless exciting shades of grey. Here, in an angora blend, is a flattering heathery shade, styled in a cozy oversized boatneck. This is a large-needle project with the added interest of five easy cables on the front and on the back, adding texture and interest to the simple design. The back and the front are exactly the same; the sleeves are plainly knit in basic stockinette; the feeling is so soft, warm, and luxurious.

Design Tip

It's a pleasure to knit with a blend of angora and nylon yarn. I chose heather grey for this design to make sure that the cables on the front and back would be visible, although the long hairs of the angora keep the cables looking subtle. Other flattering colors for this style would be pure white, pale aqua, bright rose, or cornflower blue.

Sizes

Small (medium, large)

Finished Measurements

42 (44, 46) inches (106.5, 112, 117 cm)

Materials

Approx. 1023 (1116, 1209) yards (935.5, 1020.5, 1105.5 m) of 50% angora/50% nylon yarn, worsted weight
Knitting needles in Size 9 U.S. (5.5 mm)
Cable needle
Tapestry needle for sewing seams

Gauge

16.8 stitches and 21 rows = 4 inches (10 cm) cabled pieces
16 stitches and 21 rows = 4 inches (10 cm) stockinette pieces
Always take time to check your gauge.

Pattern Stitches

Stockinette
Row 1: Knit, right side.
Row 2: Purl, wrong side.

Cables: There are 5 cables on front and back; cable instructions are included below.

Rib
Row 1: K1, p1. Repeat row 1.

Back

Cast on 88 (92, 96) sts. K1, p1 rib for 1¼ inches (3 cm).
Begin pattern as follows:
Row 1: K8 (10, 12), *p1, k6, p1, k8; repeat from * but end k8 (10, 12).
Row 2: P 8 (10, 12), *k1, p6, k1, p8; repeat from * but end p8 (10, 12).
Row 3: As row 1.
Row 4: As row 2.
Row 5: As row 1.
Row 6: As row 2.
Row 7: As row 1, except twist the cables on each knit 6 (slip 3 sts onto a cable needle and hold in back of work; knit the next 3 sts from the left hand needle; then, knit the sts from the cable needle).

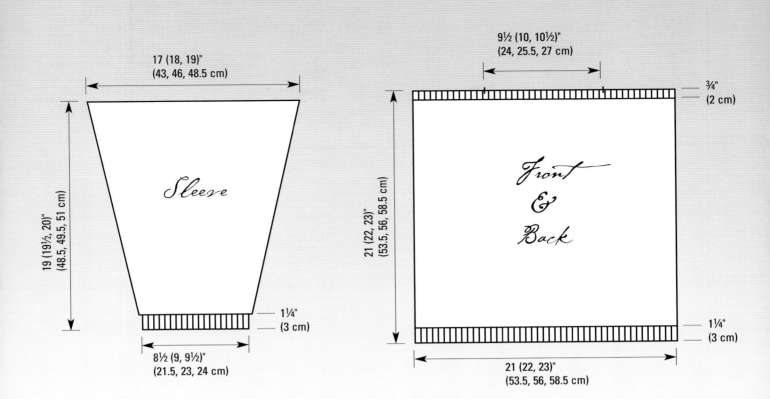

Sleeve

17 (18, 19)"
(43, 46, 48.5 cm)

19 (19½, 20)"
(48.5, 49.5, 51 cm)

1¼"
(3 cm)

8½ (9, 9½)"
(21.5, 23, 24 cm)

Front & Back

9½ (10, 10½)"
(24, 25.5, 27 cm)

¾"
(2 cm)

21 (22, 23)"
(53.5, 56, 58.5 cm)

1¼"
(3 cm)

21 (22, 23)"
(53.5, 56, 58.5 cm)

Row 8: As row 2.

Repeat this 8-row pattern to 20¼ (21¼, 22¼) inches (51.5, 54, 56.5 cm).

Then, k1, p1 rib for 3/4 inch (2 cm). Bind off.

Front

Work same as back.

Sleeves

Cast on 34 (36, 38) sts. K1, p1 rib for 1¼ inches (3 cm).

Work in stockinette, increasing 1 st each side every 6th row, to 19 (19½, 20) inches (48.5, 49.5, 51 cm). Bind off.

Finishing

Sew shoulder seams, leaving a neck opening of 9½ (10, 10½) inches (24, 25.5, 27 cm).

Sew sleeve, side, and underarm seams.

This project was knitted with 11 (12, 13) balls of Reynolds Yarns' *Devotion*, color #243, 1.75 oz (50 g) = approx. 93 yards (85 m) per ball.

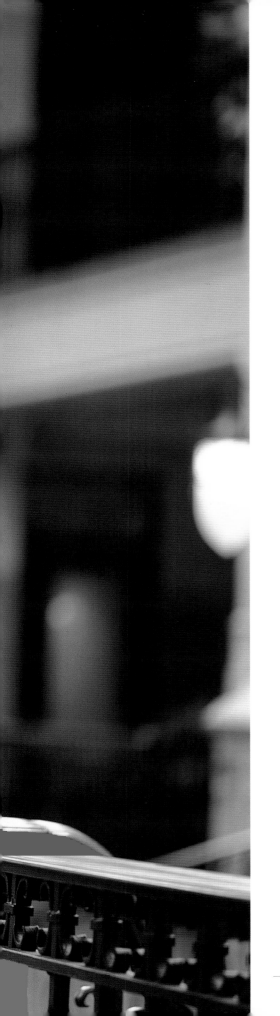

Sleeveless Black MAGIC

Y OU KNOW HOW IT FEELS—THAT TOUCH
OF SOFT VELVET. IT'S HERE, IN A
SUMPTUOUS BLACK YARN. KNIT IN
STOCKINETTE ON SMALL NEEDLES, THIS SLEEVELESS
FUNNEL NECK EVENING SWEATER HAS THE INTRICATE
TEXTURE OF A WOVEN FABRIC. A YARN WITH VISCOSE
MICROFIBERS REQUIRES SMALL NEEDLES TO PREVENT
THE YARN FROM TWISTING AS YOU KNIT AND TO
HELP THE SWEATER KEEP ITS SHAPE.

Design Tip

*B*lack velvet yarn–what a find! But this one has its idiosyncra-cies: it tends to worm and wiggle and have a life of its own. Worked on small needles, it behaves really well. Some knitters have noted that the knitted pieces tend to look biased and slightly uneven, but when it's all sewn together, the problem disappears.

Sizes

Small (medium, large)

Finished Measurements

34 (36, 38) inches (86.5, 91.5, 96.5 cm)

Materials

Approx. 480 (600, 720) yards (439, 548.5, 658.5 m) of 72% viscose microfibers/28% wool yarn, sport weight
Knitting needles in size 5 U.S. (3.75 mm)
Crochet hook size F
Tapestry needle for sewing seams

Gauge

16 sts and 20 rows = 4 inches (10 cm)
Always take time to check your gauge.

Pattern Stitches

Stockinette
Row 1: Knit, right side.
Row 2: Purl, wrong side

Garter
Row 1: Knit. Repeat row 1.

Back

Cast on 68 (72, 76) sts.
Garter stitch for $^3/_4$ inch (2 cm).
Then work in stockinette to 12$^1/_2$ (13, 13$^1/_2$) inches (32, 33, 34.5 cm).
Shape armholes: bind off 3 sts at beginning of next 2 rows; then bind off 2 sts at beginning of next 2 rows; then bind off 1 st each side every other row 3 times.
Work even until armhole measures 7$^1/_2$ (8, 8$^1/_2$) inches (19, 20.5, 21.5 cm) and total measurement is 20 (21, 22) inches (51, 53.5, 56 cm).
Then, bind off 8 (10, 12) sts at beginning of next 2 rows and continue to work in stockinette on central 36 sts for 1$^1/_2$ inches (4 cm); then, garter stitch for another $^1/_2$ inch (1.5 cm) and bind off loosely.

Front

Work same as back.

Finishing

Sew seams.
Slip-stitch loosely around armholes with crochet hook F.

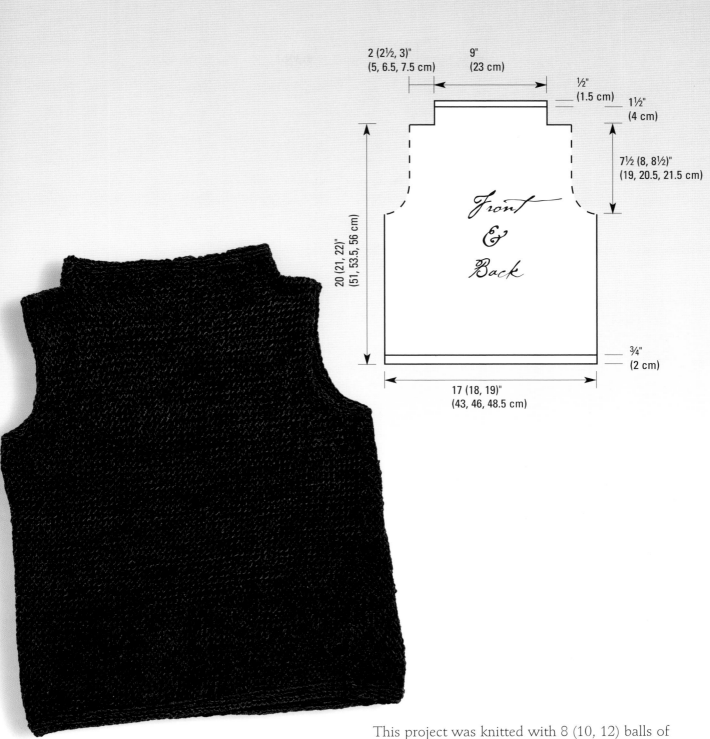

2 (2½, 3)"
(5, 6.5, 7.5 cm)

9"
(23 cm)

½"
(1.5 cm)

1½"
(4 cm)

7½ (8, 8½)"
(19, 20.5, 21.5 cm)

20 (21, 22)"
(51, 53.5, 56 cm)

Front & Back

¾"
(2 cm)

17 (18, 19)"
(43, 46, 48.5 cm)

This project was knitted with 8 (10, 12) balls of Muench Yarns' *Touch Me*, color #3607, 1.75 oz (50 g) = approx. 60 yards (55 m) per ball.

Chocolate DECADENCE

TWO OF MY FAVORITE LUXURIOUS
yarns begged to be combined,
in colors that reminded me of
a most important food group—chocolate!
One strand of thin, supersoft kid mohair
and one of shiny nylon ribbon are held
together throughout. Two strands of
ribbon are slip-stitched around the neck,
cuffs, and hem to provide the finish and
catch the light on this flattering V-neck.

Design Tip

Knitting with two different yarns held together is a unique experience. I chose a very soft kid mohair in rich chocolatey brown and a complementary nylon ribbon to knit with it. The possible color combinations are so varied, it was not easy to choose. I had made swatches of white mohair with white ribbon, black with black, red with red, grey with silver, but the browns enriched this particular design.

Sizes
Small (medium, large)

Finished Measurements
36 (40, 44) inches (91.5, 101.5, 112 cm)

Materials
Approx. 924 (1078, 1232) yards (845, 985.5, 1126.5 m) 70% super kid mohair/25% nylon/5% wool yarn, sport weight

Approx. 1001 (1144, 1287) yards (915.5, 1046, 1177 m) of 100% nylon ribbon yarn, fingering weight

Knitting needles in size 9 U.S. (5.5 mm)

Crochet hook size F

Tapestry needle for sewing seams

Gauge
18 sts and 24 rows = 4 inches (10 cm)
Always take time to check your gauge.

Pattern Stitch
Stockinette
Row 1: Knit, right side.
Row 2: Purl, wrong side.

Back
With 2 strands held together (1 mohair, 1 nylon ribbon), cast on 84 (88, 96) sts.
Row 1: Knit.
Row 2: Knit.
Row 3: Purl.
Continue in stockinette, beginning with a purl row, to 21 (22, 23) inches (53.5, 56, 58.5 cm). Bind off.

Front
Work as for back until piece measures 14 (15, 16) inches (35.5, 38, 40.5 cm) from beginning.
Next row, work 42 (44, 48) sts across and split for V, joining 2nd balls of yarn and work to end.
To decrease on first half, work to last 3 sts, then k2 together, k1.
On second half, work as follows: k1, ssk (slip 2 sts knitwise, one at a time, to right-hand needle, then insert left-hand needle into front of these 2 sts and knit them together).
Working both sides at the same time, decrease 1 st at neck edges every other row until piece measures 21 (22, 23) inches (53.5, 56, 58.5 cm). Bind off.

Sleeves
With 2 strands held together (1 mohair, 1 nylon ribbon), cast on 36 (38, 40) sts.
Row 1: Knit.
Row 2: Knit.
Row 3: Purl.
Continue in stockinette, beginning with a purl row, increasing 1 st each side every 6th row, until 18 1/2 (19, 19 1/2) inches (47, 48.5, 49.5 cm). Bind off.

Finishing
Sew shoulder seams. Sew sleeve, side, and under arm seams.
With 2 strands of nylon ribbon, using crochet hook F, slip stitch around neck, cuffs, and bottom edge.

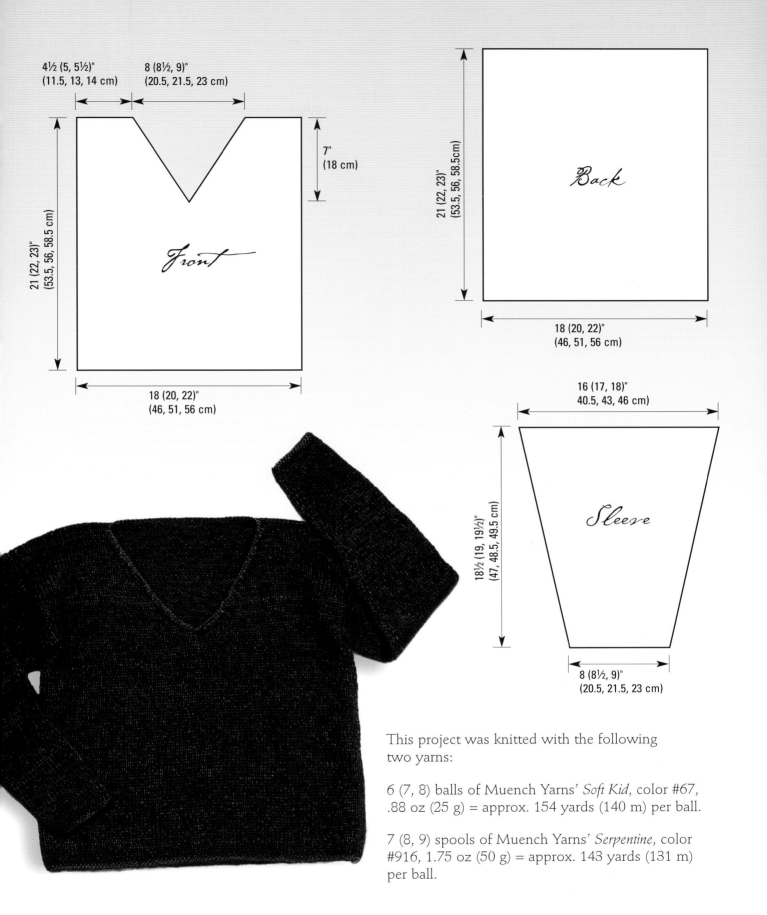

4½ (5, 5½)"
(11.5, 13, 14 cm)

8 (8½, 9)"
(20.5, 21.5, 23 cm)

7"
(18 cm)

Front

21 (22, 23)"
(53.5, 56, 58.5 cm)

18 (20, 22)"
(46, 51, 56 cm)

Back

21 (22, 23)"
(53.5, 56, 58.5cm)

18 (20, 22)"
(46, 51, 56 cm)

16 (17, 18)"
40.5, 43, 46 cm)

Sleeve

18½ (19, 19½)"
(47, 48.5, 49.5 cm)

8 (8½, 9)"
(20.5, 21.5, 23 cm)

This project was knitted with the following two yarns:

6 (7, 8) balls of Muench Yarns' *Soft Kid*, color #67, .88 oz (25 g) = approx. 154 yards (140 m) per ball.

7 (8, 9) spools of Muench Yarns' *Serpentine*, color #916, 1.75 oz (50 g) = approx. 143 yards (131 m) per ball.

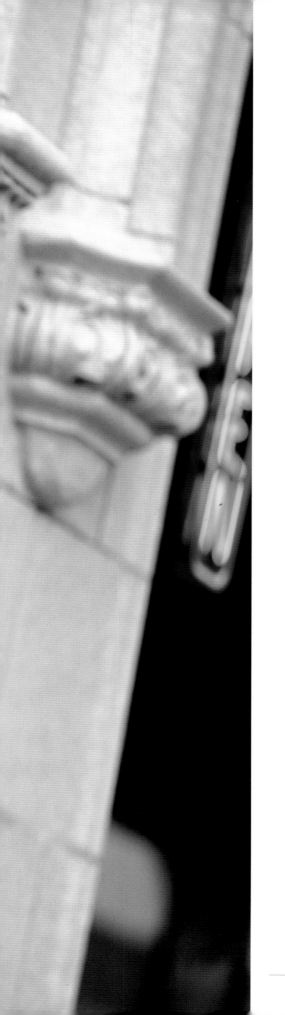

Pale Aqua
TURTLENECK

THIS SUPERSOFT MOHAIR TURTLENECK offers luxurious, lightweight warmth. It's a very quick knit on large needles, no ribbing anywhere, all stockinette stitch. The front of the sweater and its half of the turtleneck are knit in one continuous piece; same for the back. With its cozy, slightly boxy, comfortable fit, you'll wear this one again and again.

Back

Cast on 86 (90, 94) sts.

Work in stockinette to 21 (22, 23) inches (53.5, 56, 58.5 cm).

Bind off 23 (25, 27) sts at beginning of next 2 rows.

Continue in stockinette on remaining central stitches for 7¹/₂ inches (19 cm). Bind off.

Front

Work same as back.

Sleeves

Cast on 36 (38, 40) sts.

Work in stockinette, increasing 1 st each side every 5th row, to 19 (19¹/₂, 20) inches (48.5, 49.5, 51 cm). Bind off.

Finishing

Sew shoulder and turtleneck seams. Sew sleeve, underarm, and side seams.

All edges will roll.

Design Tip

*T*his sweater will need a camisole under it since it is such a fine yarn knit on relatively large needles. I have seen this sweater worn wrapped around the shoulders on a cool summer evening or as a lightweight winter turtleneck under a jacket.

Sizes

Small (medium, large)

Finished Measurements

38 (40, 42) inches (96.5, 101.5, 106.5 cm)

Materials

Approx. 924 (1078, 1232) yards (845, 985.5, 1126.5 m) of 70% super kid mohair/25% nylon/5% wool yarn, sport weight

Knitting needles in size 9 U.S. (5.5 mm)

Tapestry needle for sewing seams

Gauge

18 sts and 20 rows = 4 inches (10 cm)

Always take time to check your gauge.

Pattern Stitch

Stockinette

Row 1: Knit, right side.

Row 2: Purl, wrong side.

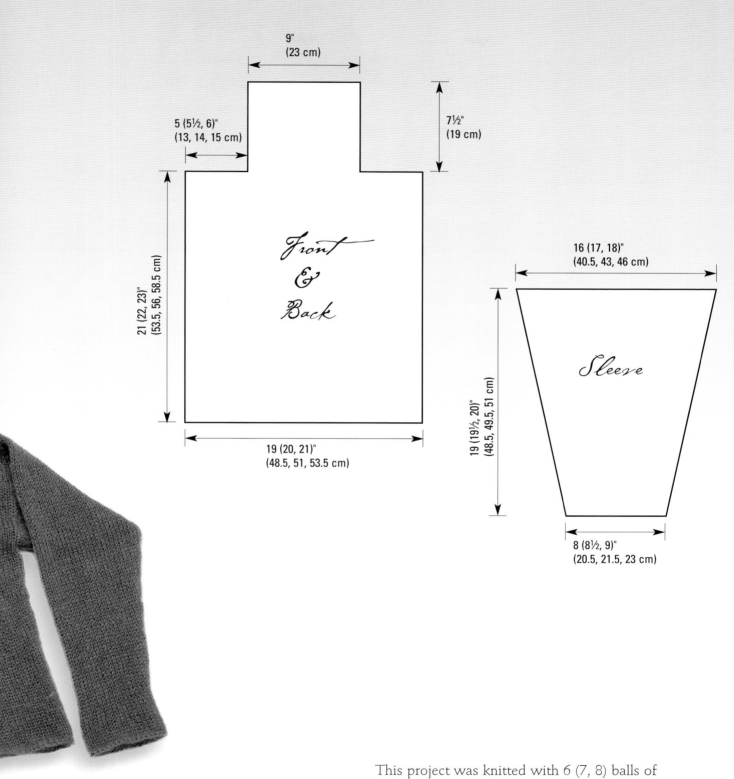

9"
(23 cm)

5 (5½, 6)"
(13, 14, 15 cm)

7½"
(19 cm)

Front
&
Back

21 (22, 23)"
(53.5, 56, 58.5 cm)

19 (20, 21)"
(48.5, 51, 53.5 cm)

16 (17, 18)"
(40.5, 43, 46 cm)

Sleeve

19 (19½, 20)"
(48.5, 49.5, 51 cm)

8 (8½, 9)"
(20.5, 21.5, 23 cm)

This project was knitted with 6 (7, 8) balls of Muench Yarns' *Soft Kid*, color #46, .88 oz (25 g) = approx. 154 yards (141 m) per ball.

Powder Blue BOATNECK

T his is the sweater you'll want to wear daily and make in other colors. The style, one of the ones my friends love the best, is a boatneck with side slits at the bottom for a comfortable, slightly oversized fit. Knit it quickly and easily on large needles in stockinette stitch.

Sizes
Small (medium, large)

Finished Measurements
41 (43, 45) inches (104, 109, 114.5 cm)

Materials
Approx. 1188 (1254, 1320) yards (1086.5, 1146.5, 1207 m) of 50% cotton/50% acrylic yarn, bulky weight
Knitting needles in size 10¹/₂ U.S. (6.5 mm)
Tapestry needle for sewing seams

Gauge
12 sts and 18 rows = 4 inches (10 cm)
Always take time to check your gauge.

Pattern Stitch
Stockinette
Row 1: Knit, right side.
Row 2: Purl, wrong side.

Back
Cast on 62 (64, 68) sts.
Work in stockinette to 22 (23, 24) inches (56, 58.5, 61 cm). Bind off.

Front
Work same as back.

Sleeves
Cast on 24 (26, 28) sts.
Work in stockinette, increasing 1 st each side every 6th row, to 19 (19¹/₂, 20) inches (48.5, 49.5, 51 cm). Bind off.

Finishing
Sew shoulder seams, leaving a 10-inch (25.5 cm) neck opening.
Sew sleeve, underarm, and side seams, leaving a slit of 1¹/₂ inches (4 cm) at bottom, each side.
Front and back neck edges will roll forward.

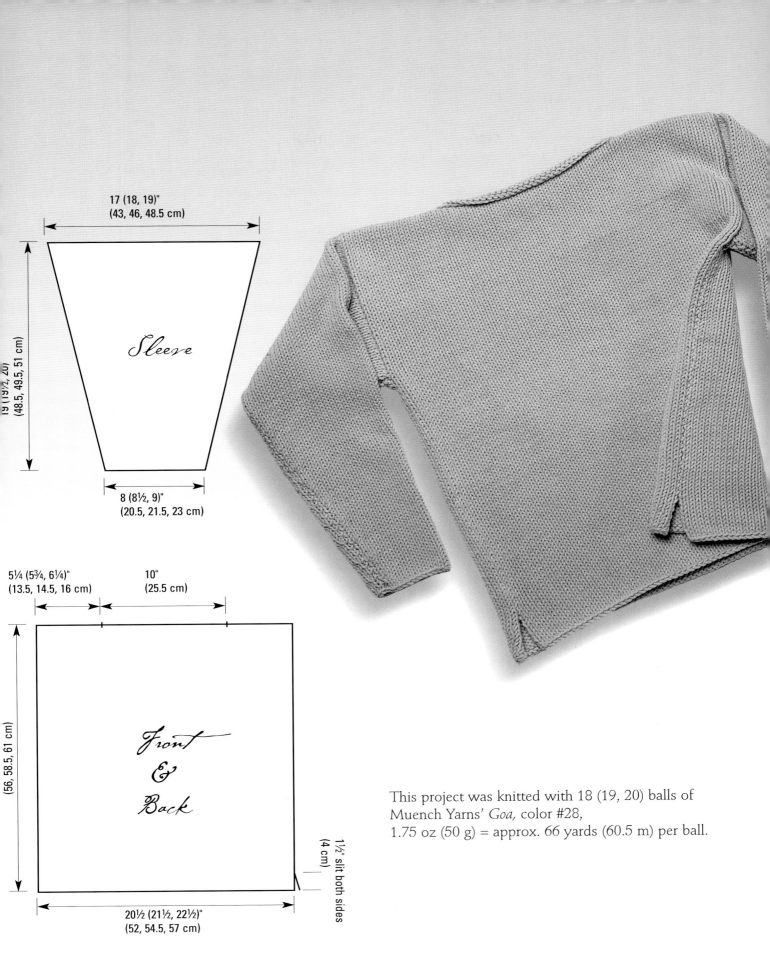

17 (18, 19)"
(43, 46, 48.5 cm)

Sleeve

19 (19½, 20)"
(48.5, 49.5, 51 cm)

8 (8½, 9)"
(20.5, 21.5, 23 cm)

5¼ (5¾, 6¼)"
(13.5, 14.5, 16 cm)

10"
(25.5 cm)

Front
&
Back

(56, 58.5, 61 cm)

1½" slit both sides
(4 cm)

20½ (21½, 22½)"
(52, 54.5, 57 cm)

This project was knitted with 18 (19, 20) balls of Muench Yarns' *Goa*, color #28, 1.75 oz (50 g) = approx. 66 yards (60.5 m) per ball.

Vibrant Red MOHAIR

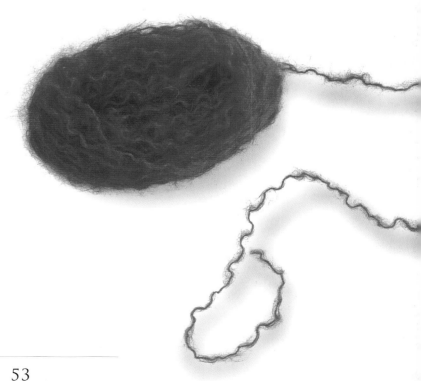

N EVERYONE'S SWEATER COLLECTION, THERE HAS TO BE AT LEAST ONE "WOW". IT COULD BE THIS LOOK-AT-ME RED MOHAIR. COMFORTABLE, ROOMY, WITH DROPPED SHOULDERS—WEAR THIS ONE WITH CASUAL OR DRESSY PANTS. IF YOU'RE A FAST KNITTER—ONE LONG WEEKEND, TWO LARGE NEEDLES, AND IT'S DONE! THERE'S NOT A RIBBING IN SIGHT.

Design Tip

*T*his is one of the first sweaters I designed. I have always loved mohair, its soft lightweight warmth, and the way it receives the color of the dyes, especially here in red. Fancy stitches are not necessary to enhance the beauty of the yarn. Only the stockinette stitch is used in the design so that the sleeve, neck, and bottom edges will all roll forward. Be sure to bind off all edges loosely or you will feel a tightness in the bound-off rows and the edges will not roll properly.

Sizes
Small (medium, large)

Finished Measurements
42 (44, 46) inches (106.5, 113, 117 cm)

Materials
Approx. 810 (900, 990) yards (740.5, 823, 905.5 m), of 76% mohair/17% wool/6% nylon yarn, bulky weight.
Knitting needles in size 11 U.S. (8 mm)
Tapestry needle for sewing seams

Gauge
12 sts and 16 rows = 4 inches (10 cm)
Always take time to check your gauge.

Pattern Stitch
Stockinette
Row 1: Knit, right side.
Row 2: Purl, wrong side.

Back
Cast on 62 (66, 70) sts.
Work in pattern to 22 (23, 24) inches (56, 58.5, 61 cm). Bind off.

Front
Work same as back.

Sleeves
Cast on 28 (30, 32) sts.
Work in pattern, increasing 1 st each side every 6th row, to 18 (19, 20) inches (46, 48.5, 51 cm). Bind off.

Finishing
Sew shoulder seams, leaving a neck opening of 10 (10½, 11) inches (25.5, 27, 28 cm).
Sew armhole, sleeve, and side seams.
All edges will roll slightly.

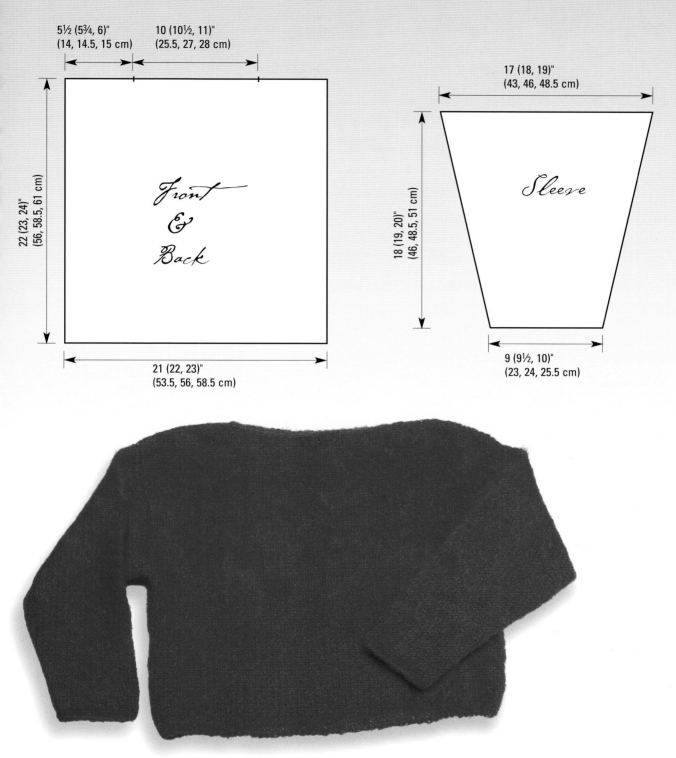

5½ (5¾, 6)"
(14, 14.5, 15 cm)

10 (10½, 11)"
(25.5, 27, 28 cm)

Front & Back

22 (23, 24)"
(56, 58.5, 61 cm)

21 (22, 23)"
(53.5, 56, 58.5 cm)

17 (18, 19)"
(43, 46, 48.5 cm)

Sleeve

18 (19, 20)"
(46, 48.5, 51 cm)

9 (9½, 10)"
(23, 24, 25.5 cm)

This project was knitted with 9 (10, 11) balls of Classic Elite Yarns' *La Gran Mohair*, color #6527, 1.5 oz (42 g) = approx. 90 yards (82.5 m) per ball.

Comfy Winter
TURTLENECK

THIS MAY BECOME YOUR FAVORITE WIN-

TER SWEATER. THE YARN IS A VERY

SOFT, THICK, EXTRA-FINE MERINO

WOOL, KNIT WITH LARGE NEEDLES IN STOCKINETTE

STITCH. A K2-P2 TWISTED RIB AT CUFFS, BOTTOM,

AND TURTLENECK COMPLETES THE CLASSIC DESIGN.

IT MAY LOOK WEIGHTY, BUT IS SURPRISINGLY LIGHT,

YET WARM TO WEAR.

Design Tip

This pattern is simple and straightforward. The ribbing at the bottom, cuffs, and turtleneck is not tight fitting, but be sure to bind off the stitches at the end of the turtleneck loosely, so it will go over your head easily and have a relaxed look. Go ahead and knit it again in red or white!

Sizes

Small (medium, large)

Finished Measurements

41 (44, 46) inches (104, 112, 117 cm)

Materials

Approx. 1056 (1188, 1320) yards (965.5, 1086.5, 1207 m) of 100% merino wool yarn, bulky weight
Knitting needles in size 11 U.S. (8 mm)
Stitch holder
Tapestry needle for sewing seams

Gauge

12 sts and 16 rows = 4 inches (10 cm)
Always take time to check your gauge.

Pattern Stitches

Stockinette
Row 1: Knit, right side.
Row 2: Purl, wrong side.

Twisted Rib
Row 1: Knit 2 (knit into the back of the knit sts), purl 2.
Row 2: Purl 2, knit 2 (knit into the back of the knit sts). Repeat.

Back

Cast on 62 (66, 70) sts. K2, p2 twisted rib for $2^{1}/_{2}$ inches (6.5 cm).
Work even in stockinette to 22 (23, 24) inches (56, 58.5, 61 cm). Bind off.

Front

Cast on 62 (66, 70) sts. K2, p2 twisted rib for $2^{1}/_{2}$ inches (6.5 cm).
Work even in stockinette to $19^{1}/_{2}$ ($20^{1}/_{2}$, $21^{1}/_{2}$) inches (49.5, 52, 54.5 cm).
For neck decrease, k24 (26, 28) sts, slip 14 sts onto holder. With second ball of yarn, k24 (26, 28) sts.
Decrease 1 st each side of neck edge every other row until front is 22 (23, 24) inches (56, 58.5, 61 cm).
Bind off.

Sleeves

Cast on 28 sts. K2, p2 twisted rib for $2^{1}/_{2}$ inches (6.5 cm).
Work in stockinette, increasing 1 st each side every 5th row, to 19 ($19^{1}/_{2}$, 20) inches (48.5, 49.5, 51 cm). Bind off.

Finishing

Sew seams. Pick up stitches around neck with same size needle and K2, p2 twisted rib for $7^{1}/_{2}$ inches (19 cm). Bind off.

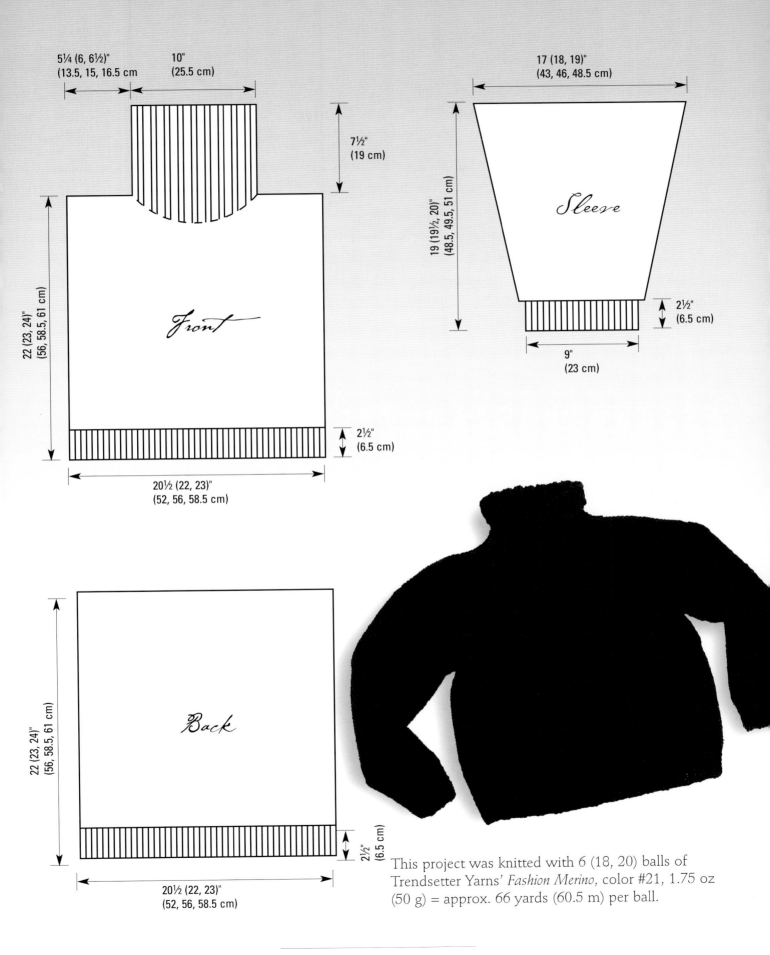

5¼ (6, 6½)"
(13.5, 15, 16.5 cm)

10"
(25.5 cm)

7½"
(19 cm)

17 (18, 19)"
(43, 46, 48.5 cm)

19 (19½, 20)"
(48.5, 49.5, 51 cm)

Sleeve

22 (23, 24)"
(56, 58.5, 61 cm)

Front

2½"
(6.5 cm)

2½"
(6.5 cm)

9"
(23 cm)

20½ (22, 23)"
(52, 56, 58.5 cm)

22 (23, 24)"
(56, 58.5, 61 cm)

Back

2½"
(6.5 cm)

20½ (22, 23)"
(52, 56, 58.5 cm)

This project was knitted with 6 (18, 20) balls of
Trendsetter Yarns' *Fashion Merino*, color #21, 1.75 oz
(50 g) = approx. 66 yards (60.5 m) per ball.

Cozy FUNNEL NECK

DECEMBER—A COLD, CRISP DAY AND IT'S TIME FOR A WALK. GRAB A FAVORITE SWEATER, MAYBE THIS NATURAL SOFT WOOL ONE YOU'VE JUST COMPLETED—THE ONE WITH THE EASY SLIP-STITCH PATTERN AND FUNNEL NECK. THE YARN IS SMOOTH AND THICK, AND IS QUICKLY KNIT ON VERY LARGE NEEDLES.

Sizes
Small (medium, large)

Finished Measurements
40 (42, 44) inches (101.5, 106.5, 112 cm)

Materials
Approx. 880 (990, 1100) yards (804.5, 905.5, 1006 m) of 100% pure new wool, bulky weight
Knitting needles in size 15 U.S. (10 mm)
Tapestry needle for sewing seams

Gauge
11 sts and 16 rows = 4 inches (10 cm)
Always take time to check your gauge.

Pattern Stitch
Slip-stitch rib (multiple of 2)
Row 1: K1, slip 1 (purlwise).
Row 2: Purl.
Repeat these 2 rows.

Back
Cast on 58 (60, 62) sts.
Work in pattern to 22 (23, 24) inches (56, 58.5, 61 cm).
Make funnel neck: bind off 16 sts at the beginning of next 2 rows. Continue pattern on central 26 (28, 30) sts for 1¹/₂ inches (4 cm).
Bind off loosely.

Front
Work same as back.

Sleeves
Cast on 22 (24, 26) sts.
Work in pattern, increasing 1 st each side every 5th row, to 19 (20, 21) inches (48.5, 51, 53.5 cm).
Bind off.

Finishing
Sew shoulder, neck, armhole, sleeve, and side seams.

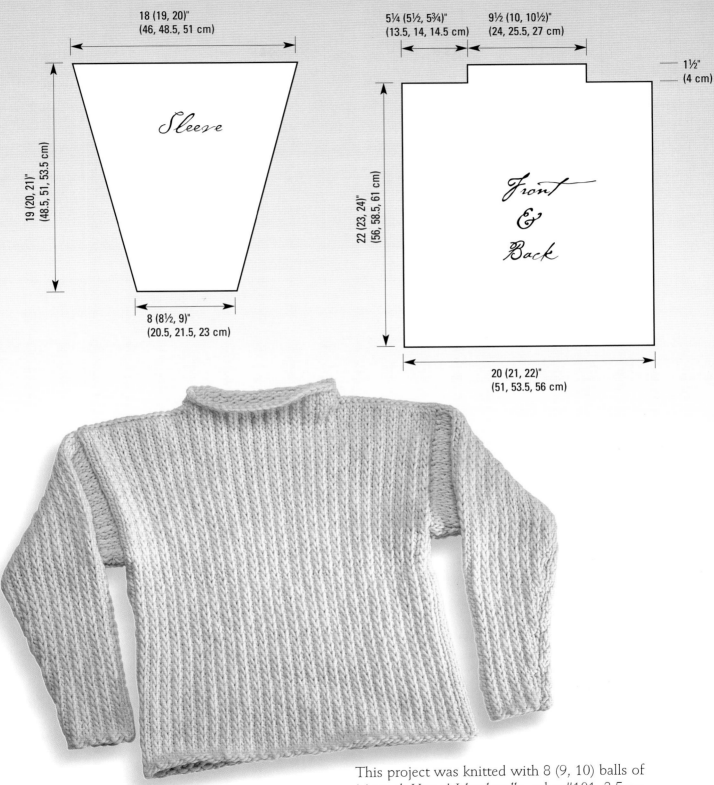

18 (19, 20)"
(46, 48.5, 51 cm)

Sleeve

19 (20, 21)"
(48.5, 51, 53.5 cm)

8 (8½, 9)"
(20.5, 21.5, 23 cm)

5¼ (5½, 5¾)"
(13.5, 14, 14.5 cm)

9½ (10, 10½)"
(24, 25.5, 27 cm)

1½"
(4 cm)

Front
&
Back

22 (23, 24)"
(56, 58.5, 61 cm)

20 (21, 22)"
(51, 53.5, 56 cm)

This project was knitted with 8 (9, 10) balls of
Muench Yarns' *Island-wolle*, color #101, 3.5 oz
(100 g) = approx. 110 yards (100.5 m) per ball.

Silvery SWEATER

THIS SILKY BOATNECK SWEATER DRAPES SOFTLY FOR A SHIMMERING AND REFINED LOOK. WEAR IT FOR A SHOW-OFF DAY, OR A SPECIAL EVENING WHEN YOU WANT TO SHINE.

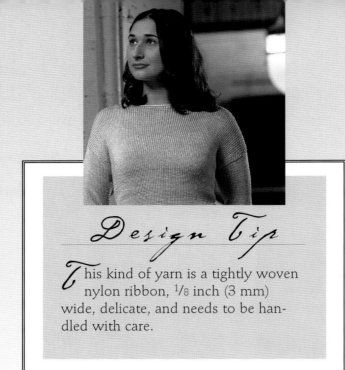

Design Tip

This kind of yarn is a tightly woven nylon ribbon, 1/8 inch (3 mm) wide, delicate, and needs to be handled with care.

Sizes

Small (medium, large)

Finished measurements

38 (40, 42) inches (96.5, 101.5, 106.5 cm)

Materials

Approx. 1287 (1430, 1573) yards (1177, 1307.5, 1438.5 m) of 100% nylon ribbon yarn, fingering weight

Knitting needles in size 4 U.S. (3.5 mm)

Tapestry needle for sewing seams

Gauge

26 sts and 38 rows = 4 inches (10 cm)

Always take time to check your gauge.

Pattern Stitches

Stockinette

Row 1: Knit, right side.

Row 2: Purl, wrong side.

Rib

Row 1: k1, p1. Repeat row 1.

Back

Cast on 124 (130, 136) sts.

K1, p1 rib for 1/2 inch (1.5 cm).

Work in stockinette to 20 (21, 22) inches (51, 53.5, 56 cm). Bind off.

Front

Work same as back.

Sleeves

Cast on 52 (56, 58) sts.

Work in stockinette, increasing 1 st each side every 7th row, to 18 1/2 (19 1/2, 20) inches (47, 49.5, 51 cm).

Bind off.

Finishing

Sew shoulder seams, leaving a neck opening of 10 (10 1/2, 11) inches (25.5, 27, 28 cm).

Sew armhole, side, and sleeve seams.

Neck and cuff edges will roll.

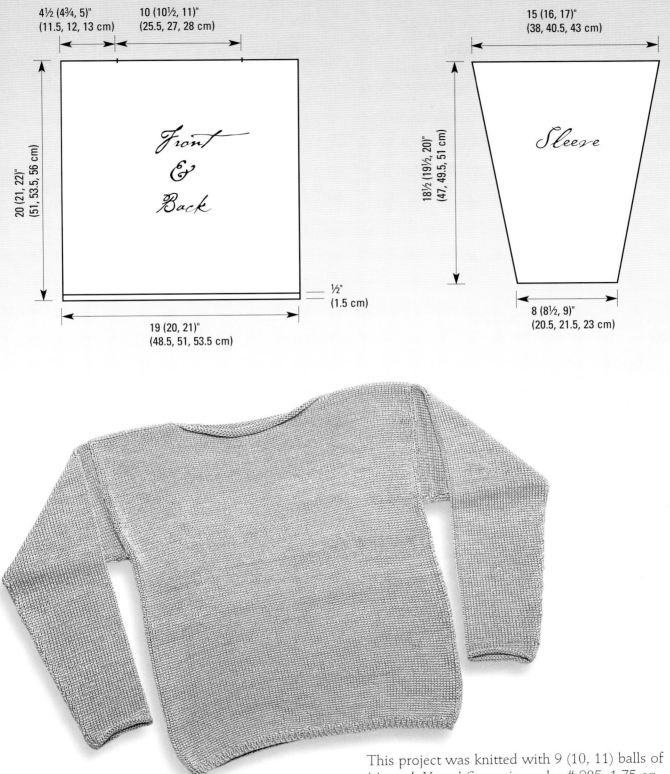

4½ (4¾, 5)"
(11.5, 12, 13 cm)

10 (10½, 11)"
(25.5, 27, 28 cm)

Front
&
Back

20 (21, 22)"
(51, 53.5, 56 cm)

½"
(1.5 cm)

19 (20, 21)"
(48.5, 51, 53.5 cm)

15 (16, 17)"
(38, 40.5, 43 cm)

Sleeve

18½ (19½, 20)"
(47, 49.5, 51 cm)

8 (8½, 9)"
(20.5, 21.5, 23 cm)

This project was knitted with 9 (10, 11) balls of Muench Yarns' *Serpentine*, color # 905, 1.75 oz (50 g) = approx. 143 yards (131 m) per ball.

Regal FUNNEL NECK

AUTUMN IS IN THE AIR—COOL, CRISP SWEATER-WEATHER DAYS. IT'S TIME TO KNIT THIS FUNNEL NECK PULLOVER FROM A SOFT, MEDIUM-WEIGHT WOOL AND RAYON YARN, THE COLOR OF A CABERNET SAUVIGNON WINE. THE STITCH IS A SIMPLE STOCKINETTE, KNIT ON LARGE NEEDLES, AND THE STYLE IS SLIGHTLY FITTED. ONE SIMPLE, WIDE CABLE RUNNING UP EACH SLEEVE PROVIDES ADDED INTEREST AND TEXTURE TO THE DESIGN.

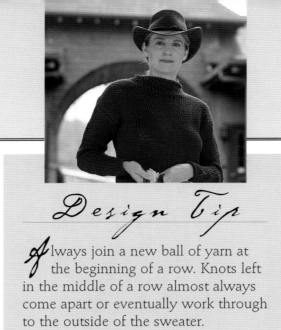

Sizes

Small (medium, large)

Finished Measurements

39 (41, 44) inches (99, 104, 112 cm)

Materials

Approx. 693 (792, 891) yards (633.5, 724, 814.5 m) of 50% wool/50% viscose yarn, bulky weight
Knitting needles in size 11 U.S. (8 mm)
Cable needle
Tapestry needle for sewing seams

Gauge

10 sts and 16 rows = 4 inches (10 cm)
Always take time to check your gauge.

Pattern Stitch

Stockinette
Row 1: Knit, right side.
Row 2: Purl, wrong side.
Cabled sleeves: see instructions below.

Back

Cast on 48 (52, 56) sts.
Work in stockinette until piece measures 22 (23, 24) inches (56, 58.5, 61 cm).
Bind off 14 (15, 16) sts at beginning of next 2 rows.
Continue in stockinette on central 20 (22, 24) sts for 1½ inches (4 cm). Bind off.

Front

Work same as back.

Sleeves

Cast on 22 (22, 24) sts.
Work in stockinette, increasing 1 st each side every 8th row, and at the same time, on the 11th row, and every following 12th row, make a central 6-stitch cable (holding 3 stitches in back on cable needle, knit the next 3, knit the 3 stitches from the holder).
Continue working to 19 (19½, 20) inches (48.5, 49.5, 51 cm). Bind off.

Finishing

Sew shoulder and neck seams; sew sleeve, side, and underarm seams.

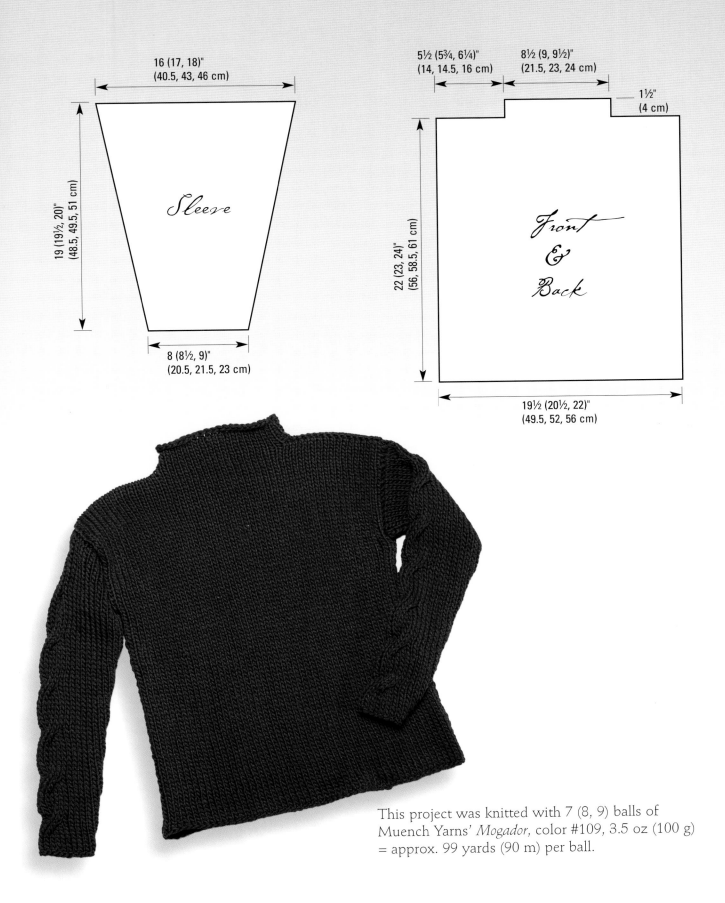

16 (17, 18)"
(40.5, 43, 46 cm)

Sleeve

19 (19½, 20)"
(48.5, 49.5, 51 cm)

8 (8½, 9)"
(20.5, 21.5, 23 cm)

5½ (5¾, 6¼)"
(14, 14.5, 16 cm)

8½ (9, 9½)"
(21.5, 23, 24 cm)

1½"
(4 cm)

Front
&
Back

22 (23, 24)"
(56, 58.5, 61 cm)

19½ (20½, 22)"
(49.5, 52, 56 cm)

This project was knitted with 7 (8, 9) balls of Muench Yarns' *Mogador*, color #109, 3.5 oz (100 g) = approx. 99 yards (90 m) per ball.

Exquisite LATTICE CABLES

THIS SWEATER IS A MILD CHALLENGE— MILD, BECAUSE THE BACK AND FRONT OF THE BOATNECK STYLE ARE THE SAME; A CHALLENGE, BECAUSE OF THE SMALL CABLES THROUGHOUT. IT'S A TIME-CONSUMING PROJECT, BUT NOT DIFFICULT AND THE MELON COLOR OF THE SOFT MERINO WOOL WILL BRIGHTEN ANY DARK WINTER DAY.

Eyelet Rib

K NITTING THE LACY
PATTERN IN THIS
FINE 100 PERCENT
MERCERIZED COTTON TAKES TIME,
BUT THE HOURS GO QUICKLY AND
SMOOTHLY BECAUSE THE STITCH
FLOWS SO EASILY. IT'S A BASIC
TWO-ROW RIB PATTERN, KNIT ON
SMALL NEEDLES THAT STABILIZE
THE MATERIAL. THE ONLY
INCREASING IS ON THE SLEEVES.
THE FRONT AND BACK ARE PRAC-
TICALLY TWO SQUARES.

EXQUSITE LATTICE CABLES

Design Tip

Some knitters love to knit two or three different sweaters at the same time, especially if one of them has an intricate and repetitive pattern, as in this cable design. To rest their eyes from the focus of small cabling, they'll switch to a simple sweater in a stockinette or garter stitch.

Sizes
Small (medium, large)

Finished Measurements
38 (40, 42) inches (96.5,101.5, 106.5 cm)

Materials
Approx. 1496 (1632, 1768) yards (1368, 1492.5, 1616.5 m) of 100% merino wool yarn, worsted weight
Knitting needles in size 7 U.S. (4.5 mm)
Cable needle
Tapestry needle for sewing seams

Gauge
26 sts and 28 rows = 4 inches (10 cm)
Always take time to check your gauge.

Pattern Stitches
Cable
Multiple of 6, plus 1 edge st each side.
Row 1: Knit.
Row 2: Purl.
Row 3: K3, * c4b, k2*. Repeat between * *, ending row with knit 3.

(C4b = slip next 2 sts onto cable needle and hold in back of work, knit the next 2 sts from left-hand needle, then knit the sts from the cable needle.)
Row 4: Purl.
Row 5: K1, *c4f, k2*. Repeat between * *, ending row c4f, k1.
(C4f = slip next 2 sts onto cable needle and hold in front of work, knit the next 2 sts from the left-hand needle, then knit the sts from the cable needle.)
Row 6: Purl.
Repeat rows 3 through 6 throughout.

Rib
Row 1: k1, p1. Repeat row 1.

Back
Cast on 126 (132, 138) sts. K1, p1 rib for 1¼ inches (3 cm).
Work in cable to 21 (22, 23) inches (53.5, 56, 58.5 cm). Bind off.

Front
Work same as back.

76

Sleeves

Cast on 54 (56, 60) sts.

Work in cable, increasing 1 st each side every 5th
   row, to 19 (19½, 20) inches (48.5, 49.5, 51
   cm). Bind off.

Finishing

Sew shoulder seams, leaving a 10-inch (25.5 cm)
   neck opening.

Sew sleeve, side and underarm seams.

Neck edges and cuffs will roll.

4½ (5, 5½)"
(11.5, 13, 14 cm)

10"
(25.5 cm)

21 (22, 23)"
(53.5, 56, 58.5 cm)

*Front
&
Back*

1¼"
(3 cm)

19 (20, 21)"
(48.5, 51, 53.5 cm)

16 (17, 18)"
(40.5, 43, 46 cm)

19 (19½, 20)"
(48.5, 49.5, 51 cm)

Sleeve

8 (8½, 9)"
(20.5, 21.5, 23 cm)

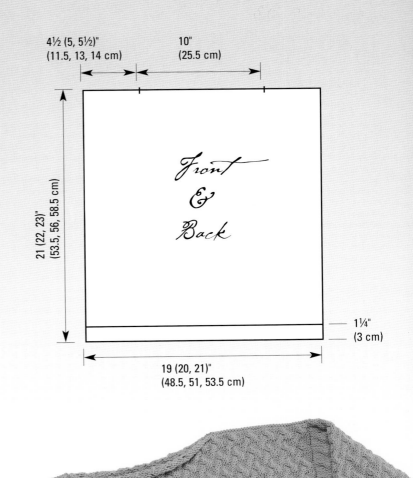

This project was knitted with 11 (12, 13) balls of
Joseph Galler Yarns' *Plassard Merino King*, color
#034, 1.75 oz (50 g) = approx. 136 yards (124.5 m)
per ball.

FINEST COTTON EYELET RIB

Design Tip

This yarn is a fine, silky cotton. Since the stitch is a lacy, stretchy eyelet rib, be sure to make a large swatch of this pattern and measure it carefully for the gauge required. You might need to go down a needle size if you knit with a loose tension, or go up a needle size if your tension is tight.

Sizes
Small (medium, large)

Finished Measurements
40 (42, 44) inches (101.5, 106.5, 112 cm)

Materials
Approx. 2055 (2192, 2329) yards (1879, 2004, 2130 m) of 100% mercerized cotton, fingering weight
Knitting needles in size 4 U.S. (3.5 mm)
Tapestry needle for sewing seams

Gauge
25 sts and 20 rows = 4 inches (10 cm)
Always take time to check your gauge.

Pattern Stitches
Eyelet Rib Stitch (over a multiple of 6 + 2)
Row 1: *P2, k2 together, yo (yarn over), k2. Repeat from *, end p2.
Row 2: K2, *p2 together, yo, p2. Repeat from *, end k2.
Repeat these 2 rows throughout.

Rib
Row 1: K1, p1. Repeat row 1.

Back
Cast on 128 (134, 140) sts.
K1, p1 rib for ½ inch (1.5 cm).
Work in eyelet until piece measures 21 (22, 23) inches (53.5, 56, 58.5 cm). Bind off.

Front
Work same as back.

Sleeves
Cast on 50 (50, 56) sts.
Work in eyelet, increasing 1 st each side every 5th row, to 19 (19½, 20) inches (48.5, 49.5, 51 cm).
Bind off.

Finishing
Sew shoulder seams, leaving an 11-inch (28 cm) neck opening.
Sew sleeve, side, and underarm seams.

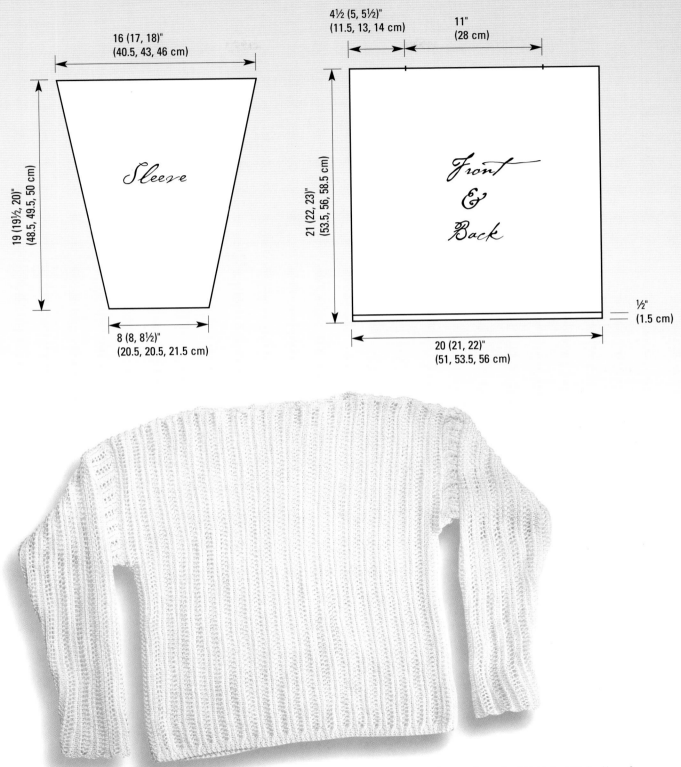

16 (17, 18)"
(40.5, 43, 46 cm)

Sleeve

19 (19½, 20)"
(48.5, 49.5, 50 cm)

8 (8, 8½)"
(20.5, 20.5, 21.5 cm)

4½ (5, 5½)"
(11.5, 13, 14 cm)

11"
(28 cm)

Front
&
Back

21 (22, 23)"
(53.5, 56, 58.5 cm)

½"
(1.5 cm)

20 (21, 22)"
(51, 53.5, 56 cm)

This project was knitted with 15 (16, 17) balls of Muench Yarns' *Roma*, color #3, 1.75 oz (50 g) = approx. 137 yards (125.5 m) per ball

Quintessential CARDIGAN

IT TOOK A WHILE TO FIND MY WAY TO THE ULTIMATE CARDIGAN STYLE. THERE ARE NO RIBBINGS, NO FRONT BANDS, NO BUTTONS, NO SET-IN SLEEVES. IT'S THE CARDIGAN IN ITS PUREST FORM AND VERY SIMPLE TO KNIT IN STOCKINETTE, WITH THE FIRST THREE ROWS OF EACH PIECE IN A KNIT, KNIT, PURL COMBINATION TO PREVENT ROLLING. THE ONLY FINISHING TOUCHES NEEDED ARE SLIP-STITCHING AROUND THE FRONT AND NECK EDGES AND A LIGHT PRESSING WITH A STEAM IRON.

Sizes
Small (medium, large)

Finished Measurements
44 (48, 52) inches (112, 122, 132 cm)

Materials
For cardigan
Approx. 756 (819, 882) yards (691.5, 749, 806.5 m)
   of 50% fine merino/50% microfiber yarn, bulky
   weight
For scarf
Approx. 252 yards (230.5 m) of 50% fine
   merino/50% microfiber yarn, bulky weight
Knitting needles
Size 13 U.S. (9 mm) for cardigan
Size 15 U.S. (10 mm) for scarf
Crochet hook size H
Tapestry needle for sewing seams

Gauge
10 sts and 14 rows = 4 inches (10 cm) for cardigan
Always take time to check your gauge.

Pattern Stitches
Stockinette (for cardigan)
Row 1: Knit, right side.
Row 2: Purl, wrong side.

Garter (for scarf)
Knit every row.

Note: Each piece begins with: Row 1: Knit, Row 2: Knit, Row 3: Purl, to keep edges from rolling. Pressing with a steam iron on the wrong side when the cardigan is complete will provide a professional-looking finish.

Back
Cast on 56 (60, 64) sts.
Row 1: Knit.
Row 2: Knit.
Row 3: Purl.
Continue in stockinette to 26 (27, 28) inches (66, 68.5, 71 cm). Bind off.

Right front
Cast on 28 (30, 32) sts.
Row 1: Knit.
Row 2: Knit.
Row 3: Purl.
Continue in stockinette to 23 (24, 25) inches (58.5, 61, 63.5 cm).
To shape neck: bind off 5 sts at beginning of right edge. Continue to work, binding off 1 st at neck edge every other row to 26 (27, 28) inches (66, 68.5, 71 cm)
Bind off.

Left front
Work as right front, but reverse shaping.

Sleeves
Cast on 28 (28, 30) sts.
Row 1: Knit.
Row 2: Knit.
Row 3: Purl.
Continue in stockinette, increasing 1 st each side every 7th row, to 19 (20, 21) inches (48.5, 51, 53.5 cm).
Bind off.

Scarf
Cast 18 sts onto size 15 needles.
Garter stitch to 68 inches (172.5 cm).
Bind off.

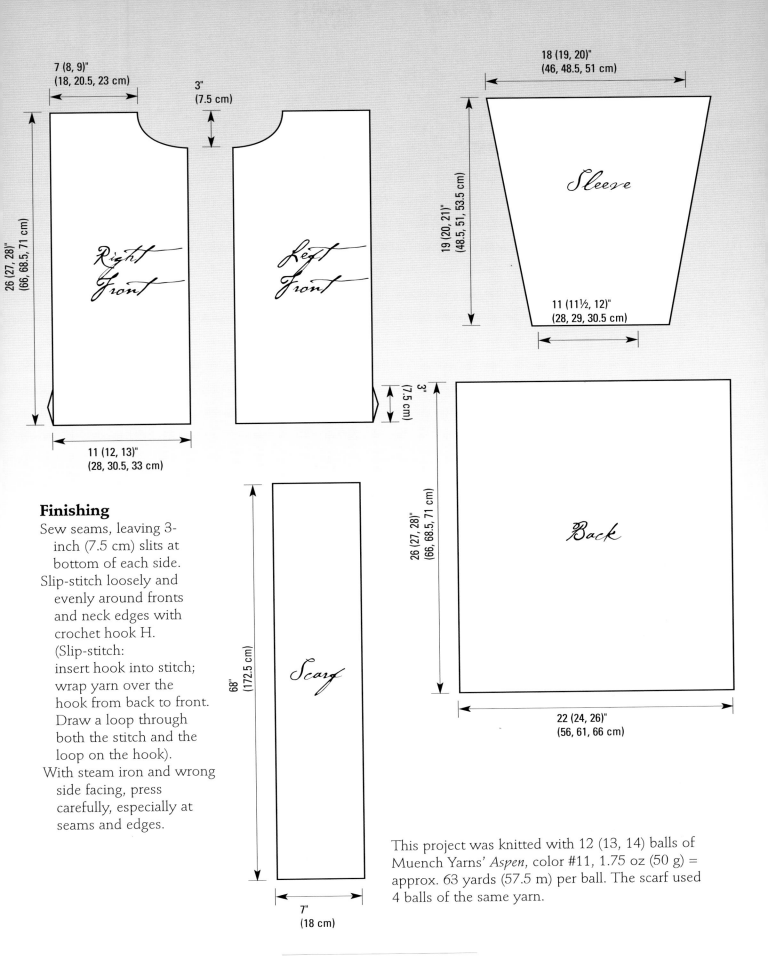

7 (8, 9)"
(18, 20.5, 23 cm)

3"
(7.5 cm)

26 (27, 28)"
(66, 68.5, 71 cm)

Right Front

Left Front

11 (12, 13)"
(28, 30.5, 33 cm)

3"
(7.5 cm)

18 (19, 20)"
(46, 48.5, 51 cm)

Sleeve

19 (20, 21)"
(48.5, 51, 53.5 cm)

11 (11½, 12)"
(28, 29, 30.5 cm)

26 (27, 28)"
(66, 68.5, 71 cm)

Back

22 (24, 26)"
(56, 61, 66 cm)

68" (172.5 cm)

Scarf

7"
(18 cm)

Finishing

Sew seams, leaving 3-inch (7.5 cm) slits at bottom of each side.

Slip-stitch loosely and evenly around fronts and neck edges with crochet hook H. (Slip-stitch: insert hook into stitch; wrap yarn over the hook from back to front. Draw a loop through both the stitch and the loop on the hook).

With steam iron and wrong side facing, press carefully, especially at seams and edges.

This project was knitted with 12 (13, 14) balls of Muench Yarns' *Aspen*, color #11, 1.75 oz (50 g) = approx. 63 yards (57.5 m) per ball. The scarf used 4 balls of the same yarn.

Café Au Lait SLEEVELESS

A CREAMY COFFEE-HUED YARN WAS SPUN INTO A FEATHER-WEIGHT 1/4-INCH-WIDE (6 MM) TAPE OF MERINO WOOL WITH A TOUCH OF NYLON. THE APPEALING SOFT TEXTURE OF THE YARN IS CAPTURED WITH VERY LARGE NEEDLES IN A BASIC STOCKINETTE STITCH. IT WILL TAKE JUST A FEW HOURS TO KNIT THIS SLEEVELESS BOATNECK; THE FRONT AND BACK ARE THE SAME.

Sizes
Small (medium, large)

Finished Measurements
34 (36, 38) inches (86.5, 91.5, 96.5 cm)

Materials
Approx. 340 (425, 510) yards (311, 388.5, 466.5 m)
  of 90% wool/10% nylon), bulky weight
Knitting needles in size 17 U.S. (12.75 mm)
Tapestry needle for sewing seams

Gauge
9 sts and 12 rows = 4 inches (10 cm)
Always take time to check your gauge.

Pattern Stitch
Stockinette
Row 1: Knit, right side.
Row 2: Purl, wrong side.

Back
Cast on 38 (40, 42) sts.
Work in stockinette to 19$\frac{1}{2}$ (20$\frac{1}{2}$, 22) inches
  (49.5, 52, 56 cm). Bind off.

Front
Work same as back.

Finishing
Sew shoulder seams, leaving a neck opening of 10
  (10$\frac{1}{2}$, 11) inches (25.5, 27, 28 cm).
Sew side seams, leaving armhole openings of 8 (8,
  8$\frac{1}{2}$) inches (20.5, 20.5, 21.5 cm).

This project was knitted with 4 (5, 6) balls of
Muench Yarns' *Madonna*, color #02, 1.75 oz (50 g)
= approx. 85 yards (77.5 m) per ball.

Design Tip

*N*ote that this sweater, done on very large needles, stretches quite a bit horizontally, but will get right back to its appropriate size with a vertical tug from top to bottom.

3½ (3¾, 4)"
(9, 9.5, 10 cm)

10 (10½, 11)"
(25.5, 27, 28 cm)

8 (8, 8½)"
(20.5, 20.5, 21.5 cm)

19½ (20½, 22)"
(49.5, 52, 56 cm)

Front & Back

17 (18, 19)"
(43, 46, 48.5 cm)

Sequined
MOHAIR

TINY SEQUINS ARE HANDSEWN INTO THIS EXQUISITE YARN BY THE MANUFACTURER AND BEAUTIFULLY SPACED TO CATCH THE LIGHT IN A SUBTLE WAY. THE YARN IS VERY FINE, BUT IT WILL TAKE JUST A FEW HOURS TO KNIT THIS EVENING SWEATER ON LARGE NEEDLES—THE BACK AND FRONT ARE THE SAME. WEAR IT LOOSELY OVER A CAMISOLE AND LET IT FLOAT OVER PANTS OR SKIRT.

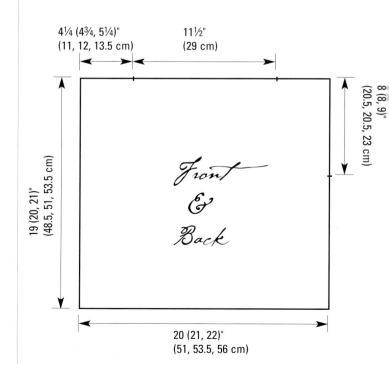

Design Tip

There is no finishing needed on this very easy-to-knit sweater. Basically, it is two knitted rectangles sewn together, leaving the appropriate openings for the neck and armholes. Bind off loosely for a soft, slightly rolled finish at the wide neckline.

Sizes
Small (medium, large)

Finished Measurements
40 (42, 44) inches (101.5, 106.5, 112 cm)

Materials
Approx. 324 (324, 432) yards (296.5, 296.5, 395 m) of mohair with sequins, fingering weight
Knitting needles in size 11 U.S. (8 mm)
Tapestry needle for sewing seams

Gauge
12 sts and 14 rows = 4 inches (10 cm)
Always take time to check your gauge.

Pattern Stitch
Stockinette
Row 1: Knit, right side.
Row 2: Purl, wrong side.

This project was knitted with 3 (3, 4) spools, Karabella Yarns' *Sequins*, color white, approx. 108 yards (99 m) per spool.

Back
Cast on 60 (64, 66) sts.
Work in stockinette until piece measures 19 (20, 21) inches (48.5, 51, 53.5 cm).
Bind off loosely.

Front
Work same as back.

Finishing
Sew shoulder seams, leaving an 11¹/₂-inch (29 cm) neck opening.
Sew side seams, leaving armhole openings of 8 (8, 9) inches (20.5, 20.5, 23 cm).

4¼ (4¾, 5¼)" (11, 12, 13.5 cm) 11½" (29 cm)

8 (8, 9)" (20.5, 20.5, 23 cm)

19 (20, 21)" (48.5, 51, 53.5 cm)

Front & Back

20 (21, 22)" (51, 53.5, 56 cm)

HOODED SWEATER

W HO SAYS A
WHOODED
SWEATER HAS
TO BE SPORTY? THIS LACY ONE,
KNIT WITH PASHMINA, THE BEST OF
CASHMERES, IS ELEGANT AND PARTY-
PERFECT. THE SIMPLE GARTER
STITCH THROUGHOUT PREVENTS
ROLLED EDGES, ELIMINATES THE
NEED FOR RIBBING, AND GIVES BODY
TO THIS LIGHTWEIGHT, SOFT YARN.

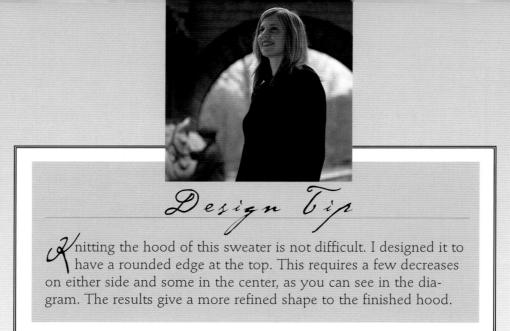

Sizes

Small (medium, large)

Finished Measurements

38 (40, 42) inches (96.5, 101.5, 106.5 cm)

Materials

Approx. 2040 (2210, 2380) yards (1865.5, 2021, 2176.5 m) of 100% cashmere yarn, sport weight
Knitting needles in size 8 U.S. (5 mm.)
Crochet hook size D
Tapestry needle for sewing seams

Gauge

20 sts and 34 rows = 4 inches (10 cm)
Always take time to check your gauge.

Pattern Stitch

Garter
Knit every row.

Back

Cast on 96 (100, 104) sts.
Slip the first stitch at the beginning of each row (for an even edge) and work garter stitch to 21 (22, 23) inches (53.5, 56, 58.5 cm).
Bind off.

Front

Work same as back to 18^1/$_2$ (19^1/$_2$, 20^1/$_2$) inches (47, 49.5, 52 cm).
Shape neck: on next row, work 39 (41, 43) sts across, join second ball of yarn and bind off 18 sts, work to end of row. Working both sides at

once, bind off 1 st at each neck edge every other row to 21 (22, 23) inches (53.5, 56, 58.5 cm).
Bind off.

Sleeves

Cast on 44 (46, 48) stitches.
Slip the first stitch at the beginning of each row (for an even edge) and work in garter stitch, increasing 1 st each side every 8th row, to 19 (19^1/$_2$, 20) inches (48.5, 49.5, 51 cm).
Bind off.

Hood

Cast on 110 sts.
Work in garter stitch (slipping the first stitch at the beginning of each row, as above), and decrease 1 stitch each side every 11th row to 110 rows (13 inches [33 cm]). But at row 85 (10 inches [25.5 cm]), knit across 55 stitches, attach second ball of yarn, work to end of row.
Work 2 rows even, then working both sides at once, decrease 1 st at each side of split (see diagram) every 3rd row to 110 rows (13 inches [33 cm]).
Bind off.

Finishing

Sew center hood seam at narrow edge (folding hood in half at central split). Sew shoulder, armhole, sleeve and side seams. Sew long edge of hood to neckline, overlapping front edges approximately ^{1}/$_2$ inch (1.5 cm).
Slip-stitch around edges of hood for even finish with crochet hook D.

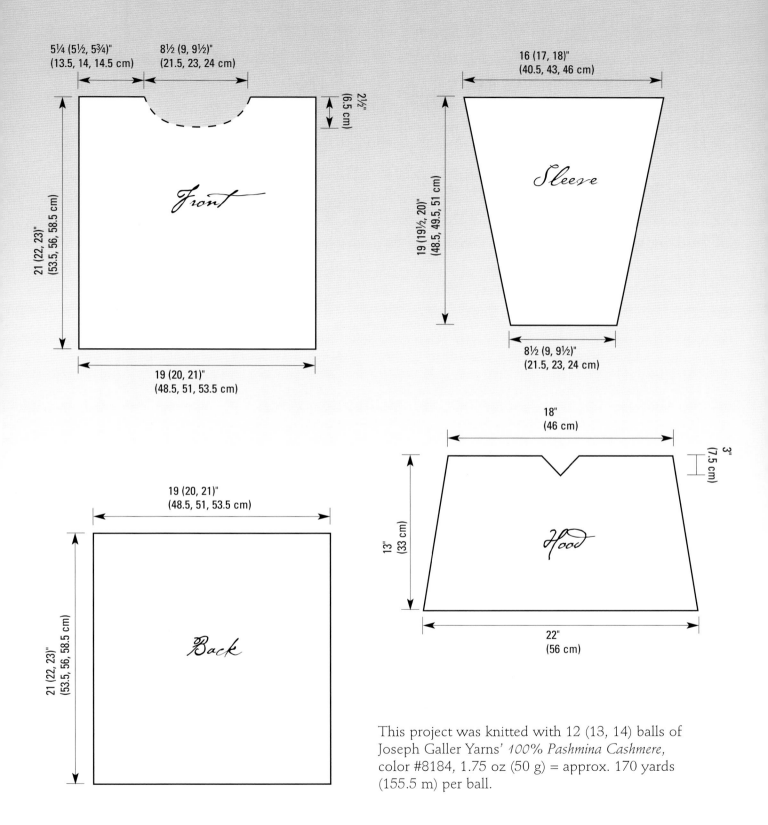

5¼ (5½, 5¾)"
(13.5, 14, 14.5 cm)

8½ (9, 9½)"
(21.5, 23, 24 cm)

2½"
(6.5 cm)

21 (22, 23)"
(53.5, 56, 58.5 cm)

Front

19 (20, 21)"
(48.5, 51, 53.5 cm)

16 (17, 18)"
(40.5, 43, 46 cm)

Sleeve

19 (19½, 20)"
(48.5, 49.5, 51 cm)

8½ (9, 9½)"
(21.5, 23, 24 cm)

19 (20, 21)"
(48.5, 51, 53.5 cm)

Back

21 (22, 23)"
(53.5, 56, 58.5 cm)

18"
(46 cm)

3"
(7.5 cm)

13"
(33 cm)

Hood

22"
(56 cm)

This project was knitted with 12 (13, 14) balls of Joseph Galler Yarns' *100% Pashmina Cashmere*, color #8184, 1.75 oz (50 g) = approx. 170 yards (155.5 m) per ball.

Perfect
TURTLENECK

W E'VE ALL BEEN LOOK-ING FOR THAT PER-FECT TURTLENECK— A FIT THAT'S NOT TOO TIGHT, NOT TOO LOOSE; A COZY, LUXURIOUS FEEL (YARN OF EXTRA-FINE MERINO WOOL COMBINED WITH SILK); AN EASY STITCH (K1, P1 RIB THROUGHOUT); AND INSTRUCTIONS THAT ARE SO SIMPLE. HERE IT IS! THIS CLASSIC SHAPE IN A CONTEMPORARY COLOR OF PALE CHARTREUSE WILL BE ONE OF YOUR FAVORITES FOR YEARS.

Sizes

Small (medium, large)

Finished Measurements

41(44, 46) inches (104, 112, 117 cm)

Materials

Approx. 1810 (1991, 2172) yards (1655, 1820.5, 1986 m) of 75% extra-fine merino wool/25% silk yarn, sport weight

Knitting needles in size 6 U.S. (4 mm)

Tapestry needle for sewing seams

Gauge

29 sts and 28 rows = 4 inches (10 cm)

Always take time to check your gauge.

Pattern Stitch

Rib

Row 1: K1, p1. Repeat row 1.

Back

Cast on 148 (158, 166) sts.

Work in pattern until piece measures 22 (23, 24) inches (56, 58.5, 61 cm).

Bind off 38 (43, 47) sts at beginning of next 2 rows.

Continue in pattern on central 72 sts for 7½ inches (19 cm). Bind off.

Front

Work same as back.

Sleeves

Cast on 62 (64, 68) sts.

Work in pattern, increasing 1 st each side every 5th row, to 20 (20½, 21) inches (51, 52, 53.5 cm). Bind off.

Finishing

Sew shoulder and turtleneck seams. Sew sleeve, side, and underarm seams.

This project was knitted with 10 (11, 12) balls of Grignasco Yarns' *Champagne*, color #595, 1.75 oz (50 g) = approx. 181 yards (165.5 m) per ball.

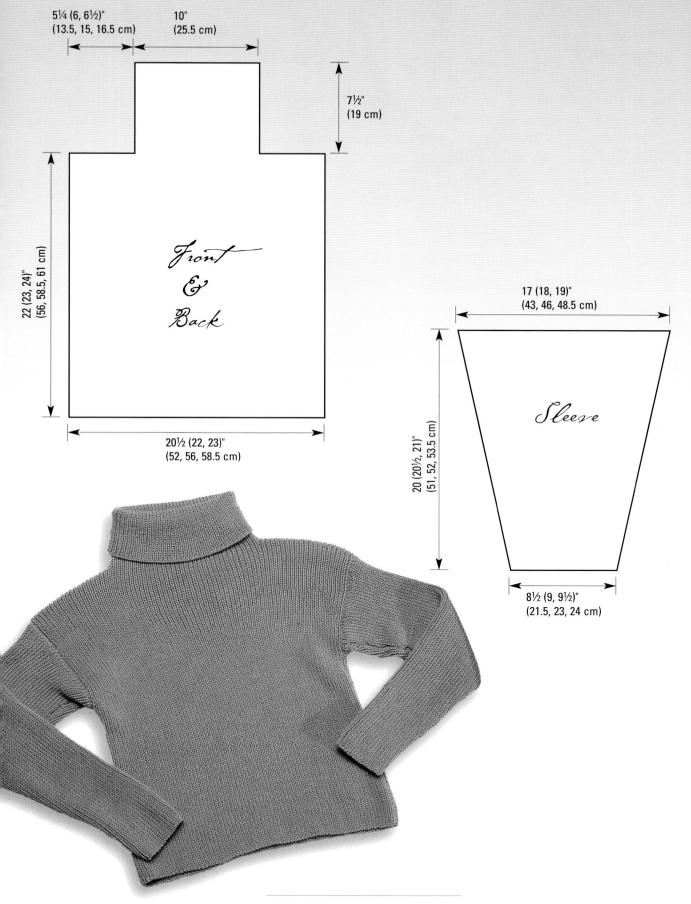

5¼ (6, 6½)"
(13.5, 15, 16.5 cm)

10"
(25.5 cm)

7½"
(19 cm)

22 (23, 24)"
(56, 58.5, 61 cm)

Front
&
Back

20½ (22, 23)"
(52, 56, 58.5 cm)

17 (18, 19)"
(43, 46, 48.5 cm)

Sleeve

20 (20½, 21)"
(51, 52, 53.5 cm)

8½ (9, 9½)"
(21.5, 23, 24 cm)

Glittery Bronze TANK TOP

THE YARN FOR THIS DESIGN IS A
TWILD ONE—A TRENDY, WIDE,
CRUNCHY RIBBON THAT IS SO
ATTENTION-GETTING, IT'S BEST TO USE ONLY
IN SMALL DOSES! THE SIMPLE BASIC TANK
TOP, WITH FRONT AND BACK KNITTED
EXACTLY THE SAME ON LARGE NEEDLES,
SUITS SUCH A GLITTERY YARN.

Design Tip

Here is an unusual ribbon yarn, ¼ inch (.25 cm) wide, which has unfinished edges that will fray softly and subtly. This is done on purpose so that, as you knit, tiny threads unravel to appear here and there throughout the fabric and become a significant part of the design. Press the finished sweater on the wrong side with a steam iron, carefully. This will soften the material and will give a more refined finish to the look.

Sizes
Small (medium, large)

Finished Measurements
32 (34, 36) inches (81.5, 86.5, 91.5 cm)

Materials
Approx. 330 (385, 440) yards (302, 352, 402.5 m) of 100% polyester ribbon yarn, bulky weight
Knitting needles in size 13 U.S. (9 mm)
Crochet hook size H
Tapestry needle for sewing seams

Gauge
13 sts and 14 rows = 4 inches (10 cm)
Always take time to check your gauge.

Pattern Stitch
Stockinette
Row 1: Knit, right side.
Row 2: Purl, wrong side.

Back
Cast on 56 (58, 62) sts.
Work in stockinette until piece measures 12 (12½, 13) inches (30.5, 32, 33 cm).
Shape armhole: bind off 3 (3, 4) sts at beginning of next 2 rows; then bind off 2 sts at beginning of next 2 rows; then, bind off 1 st at beginning of every other row 4 (4, 5) times, leaving 38 (40, 40) sts.
Work even until piece measures 3 (3½, 4) inches (7.5, 9, 10 cm) from beginning of armhole shaping.
Shape neck: k14 (14, 12), join 2nd ball of yarn, bind off 10 (12, 16) sts, k14 (14, 12). At each neck edge, bind off 1 st every other row, until back measures 20 (21, 22) inches (51, 53.5, 56 cm).
Bind off.

Front
Work same as back.

Finishing
Sew seams.
With wrong side facing and crochet hook H, slip-stitch around neck, armholes, and bottom edges.
With wrong side facing, press carefully with steam iron for a softer, flatter finish and to keep edges from rolling.

This project was knitted with 6 (7, 8) balls of Muench Yarns' *Cometa*, color #003, .88 oz (50 g) = approx. 55 yards (50.5 m) per ball.

1"
(2.5 cm)

5"
(13 cm)

8 (8½, 9)"
(20.5, 21.5, 23 cm)

20 (21, 22)"
(51, 53.5, 56 cm)

12 (12½, 13)"
(30.5, 32, 33 cm)

*Front
&
Back*

16 (17, 18)"
(40.5, 43, 46 cm)

Serene Green
WITH ONE CABLE

T his was my first experience with microfiber yarn and I was soon convinced it wouldn't be my last. To touch it is to feel a velvety, smooth finish; to work with it on large needles is to spend a few hours in quick, easy knitting. Stockinette is the chosen stitch, with a single front cable for emphasis. With the neutral, wear-with-everything pale green color, it could be an all-season sweater.

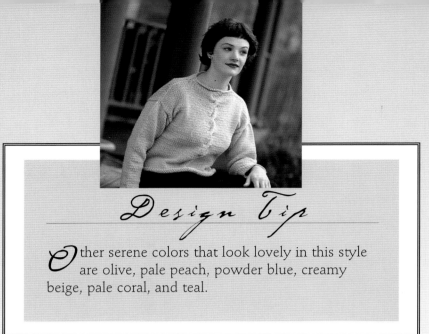

Design Tip

Other serene colors that look lovely in this style are olive, pale peach, powder blue, creamy beige, pale coral, and teal.

Sizes
Small (medium, large)

Finished Measurements
40 (43, 45) inches (101.5, 109, 114.5 cm)

Materials
Approx. 872 (959, 1046) yards (797.5 (877, 956.5 m) of 100% microfiber yarn, bulky weight
Knitting needles in size 13 U.S. (9 mm)
Cable needle
Tapestry needle for sewing seams

Gauge
20 sts and 24 rows = 6 inches (15 cm)
Always take time to check your gauge.

Pattern Stitches
Stockinette
Row 1: Knit, right side.
Row 2: Purl, wrong side.

Central cable: see instructions below.

Back
Cast on 66 (70, 74) sts.
Work in stockinette to 22 (23, 24) inches (56, 58.5, 61 cm).
Bind off 18 (20, 22) sts at beginning of next 2 rows.

On remaining 30 sts, continue in stockinette for 1³/₄ inch (4.5 cm). Bind off.

Front
Cast on 66 (70, 74) sts.
Work in stockinette for 10 rows.
On the 11th row, k29 (31, 33) sts, slip the next 4 sts onto a cable needle and hold in back, knit the next 4 sts, knit the 4 sts from the cable needle, k29 (31, 33) sts. Continue in stockinette, working cable every 12th row.
At 22 (23, 24) inches (56, 58.5, 61 cm), bind off 18 (20, 22) sts at beginning of the next 2 rows, continue in stockinette on remaining central sts and continue central cable for 1³/₄ inches (4.5 cm) more. Bind off.

Sleeves
Cast on 28 (30, 32) sts.
Work in stockinette, increasing 1 st each side every 5th row, to 19 (19¹/₂, 20) inches (48.5, 49.5, 51 cm). Bind off.

Finishing
Sew shoulder and neck seams. Sew sleeve, side, and underarm seams.

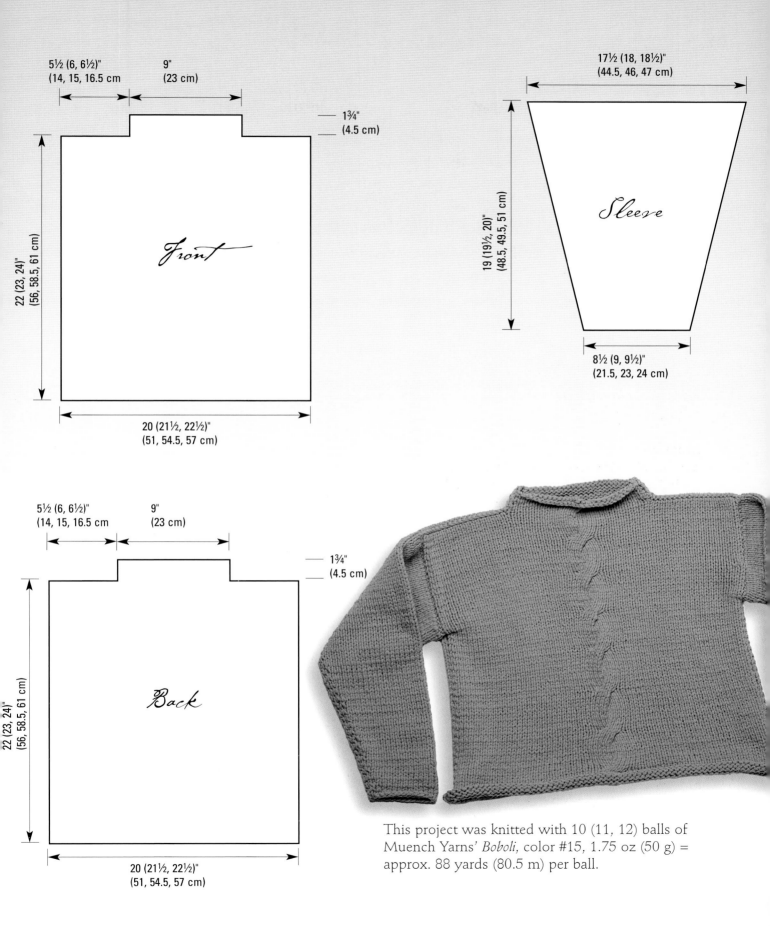

Front

5½ (6, 6½)"
(14, 15, 16.5 cm)

9"
(23 cm)

1¾"
(4.5 cm)

22 (23, 24)"
(56, 58.5, 61 cm)

20 (21½, 22½)"
(51, 54.5, 57 cm)

Sleeve

17½ (18, 18½)"
(44.5, 46, 47 cm)

19 (19½, 20)"
(48.5, 49.5, 51 cm)

8½ (9, 9½)"
(21.5, 23, 24 cm)

Back

5½ (6, 6½)"
(14, 15, 16.5 cm)

9"
(23 cm)

1¾"
(4.5 cm)

22 (23, 24)"
(56, 58.5, 61 cm)

20 (21½, 22½)"
(51, 54.5, 57 cm)

This project was knitted with 10 (11, 12) balls of Muench Yarns' *Boboli*, color #15, 1.75 oz (50 g) = approx. 88 yards (80.5 m) per ball.

Look OF LINEN

H ERE IS A GLIMMER OF SPRING IN A VISCOSE/ COTTON TAPE, WRAPPED WITH A FINE STRAND OF LINEN. THE NECKLINE IS A FLATTERING SPLIT SCOOP THAT ROLLS FORWARD AND THE SLEEVES ARE THREE-QUARTER LENGTH. THE STYLE IS SLIGHTLY BOXY, WITH AN EASY NATURAL FIT. BE SURE TO PRESS THE FINISHED SWEATER WITH A STEAM IRON (EXCEPT AROUND THE NECKLINE) FOR A SOFT, FLAT AND PROFESSIONAL LOOKING FINISH.

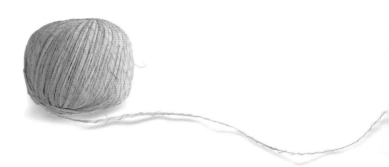

Design Tip

For those of you who like the look of linen, but not the feel of it, a blend with some linen in it would be a good solution. There's a crispy texture to the finished sweater and, in this natural color, it looks as if it has a lot of linen in it. Beautiful colors to choose from include pale melon, blush, coral, light chartreuse, deep olive, black, and white.

Sizes

Small (medium, large)

Finished Measurements

36 (38, 40) inches (91.5, 96.5, 101.5 cm)

Materials

Approx. 756 (882, 1008) yards (691.5, 806.5, 922 m) of 45% rayon/38% cotton/17% linen yarn, worsted weight
Knitting needles in size 8 U.S. (5 mm)
Crochet hook size D
Tapestry needle for sewing seams

Gauge

20 sts and 24 rows = 4 inches (10 cm)
Always take time to check your gauge.

Pattern Stitch

Stockinette
Row 1: Knit, right side.
Row 2: Purl, wrong side.
Work the first 3 rows of each piece as follows:
  Row 1: Knit.
  Row 2: Knit.
  Row 3: Purl.

Back

Cast on 90 (94, 98) sts.
Work the first 3 rows as described above.
Then, beginning with a purl row, work in stockinette to 21 (22, 23) inches (53.5, 56, 58.5 cm).
Bind off.

Front

Work same as back to 16 (17, 18) inches (40.5, 43, 46 cm).
To shape neck: Work 45 (47, 49) sts across, join 2nd ball of yarn and work to end of row. Working both sides at once, continue in stockinette for 2½ inches (6.5 cm). Then, at both neck edges, bind off 18 sts. Decrease 1 st each side of neck edge every other row to 21 (22, 23) inches (53.5, 56, 58.5) cm.
Bind off.

Sleeves

Cast on 42 (44, 46) sts.
Work the first 3 rows as described above. Then, beginning with a purl row, work in stockinette, increasing 1 st each side every 4th row, to 14 (14½, 15) inches (35.5, 37, 38 cm).
Bind off.

Finishing

Sew shoulder, armhole, sleeve, and side
   seams.

With crochet hook D, excluding the 18
   bound-off sts at each neck edge, slip-stitch
   around neck with right side facing, going
   into the front half of every other stitch. (The
   bound-off stitches at front neck edges will
   have a natural roll forward).

Press finished sweater with steam iron (except
   for the rolled neck edges), especially around
   the bottom edges for a flat professional-
   looking finish.

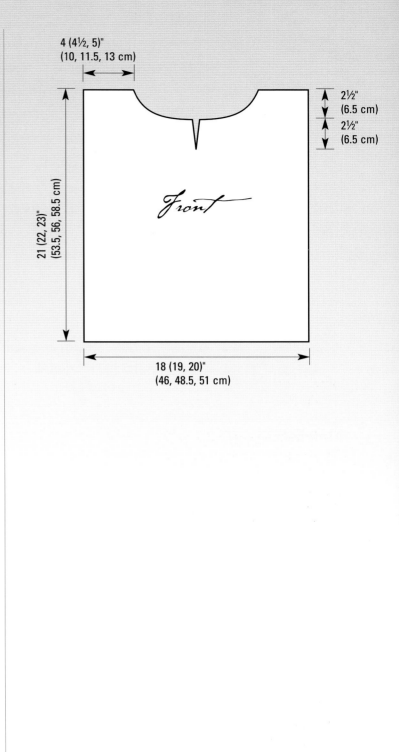

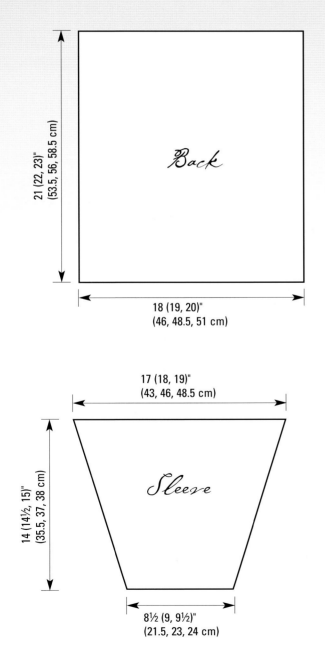

This project was knitted with 6 (7, 8) balls of
Muench Yarrns' *Bastia*, color #21, 1.75 oz (50 g) =
approx.126 yards (115 m) per ball.

Lilacs & Lace
EYELET RIB

S O SOFT, SO FEMININE, SO MUCH LIKE ONE OF MY FAVORITE FLOWERS. THOSE WERE MY THOUGHTS WHEN I SAW THIS ANGORA/WOOL YARN. I LOVE THE FEEL AND COLOR OF IT, AND WANTED TO DESIGN A ROMANTIC YET CONTEMPORARY STYLE TO SHOW IT OFF. THE STITCH IS AN EYELET RIB, LACY AND SIMPLE TO KNIT; THE STYLE IS A TIMELESS BOATNECK, EASY TO WEAR, WITH PANTS, SKIRTS, AND EVEN JEANS. WRAP, TWIST, OR KNOT THE MATCHING SCARF ANYWAY YOU LIKE TO COMPLETE THE EYE-CATCHING LOOK.

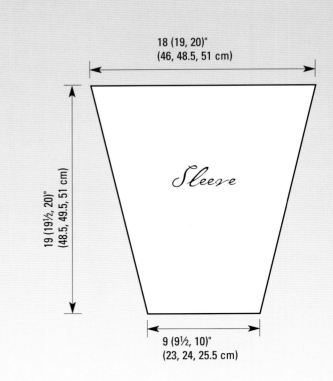

18 (19, 20)"
(46, 48.5, 51 cm)

19 (19½, 20)"
(48.5, 49.5, 51 cm)

Sleeve

9 (9½, 10)"
(23, 24, 25.5 cm)

Design Tip

*Y*ou can wear the sleeves of this sweater cuffed or uncuffed. The eyelet rib stitch looks as good on the wrong side as on the right side. When you're sewing the sleeve seams, be sure not to leave any knots at the cuff area that might show when the cuff is turned up a bit.

Sizes
Small (medium, large)

Finished Measurements
41 (45, 49) inches (104, 114, 124.5 cm)

Materials
Approx. 1392 (1479, 1566) yards (1273, 1352.5, 1432 m) of 50% extra-fine wool/33% angora/17% nylon yarn, worsted weight
Knitting needles in size 8 U. S. (5 mm)
Tapestry needle for sewing seams

Gauge
20 sts and 24 rows = 4 inches (10 cm) in pattern stitch using size 8 needles
Always take time to check your gauge.

Pattern Stitch
Eyelet rib stitch (over a multiple of 6 + 2)
Row 1: *P2, k2 tog, yo, k2. Repeat from *, end p2.
Row 2: K2, *p2 tog, yo, p2, k2. Repeat from *.

Back
Cast on 104 (112, 122) sts.
Work in pattern until piece measures 22 (23, 24) inches (56, 58.5, 61 cm). Bind off.

Front
Work same as back.

Sleeves
Cast on 44 (48, 50) sts.
Work in pattern, increasing 1 st each side every 5th row, to 19 (19½, 20) inches (48.5, 49.5, 51 cm). Bind off.

Scarf
Cast on 38 sts.
Work in pattern to 44 inches (112 cm). Bind off.

Finishing
Sew shoulder seams, leaving a neck opening of 9½ (10, 10½) inches (24, 25.5, 27 cm). Sew in sleeves (they will be long enough to cuff back).
Sew side and sleeve seams, leaving a slit opening of 1½ inches (4 cm) at bottom of each side.

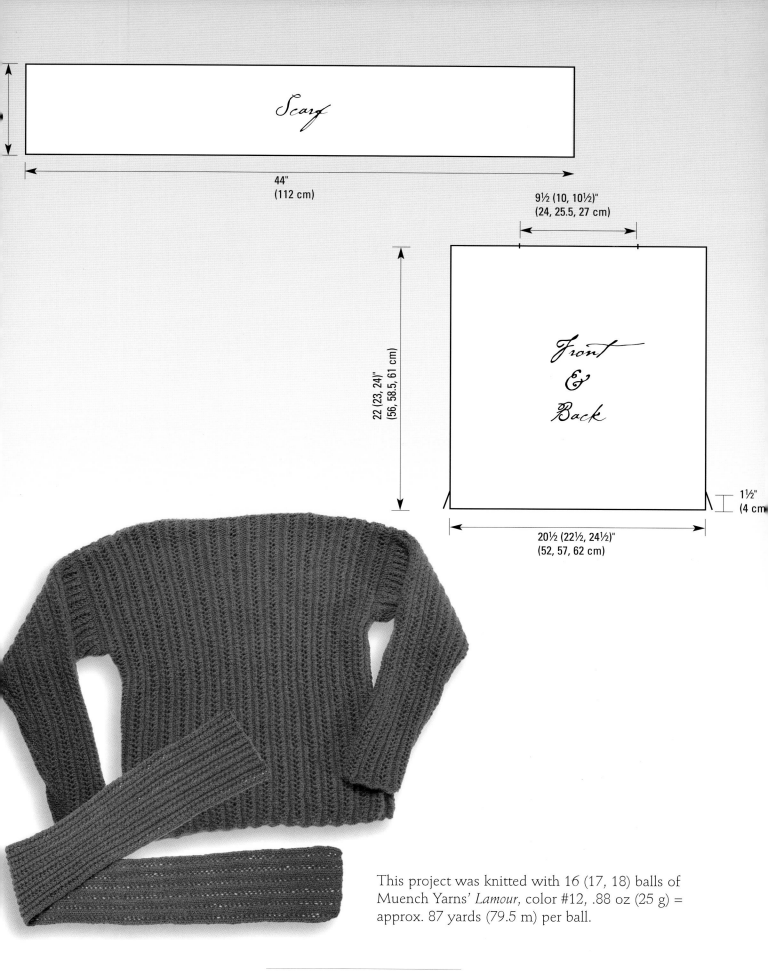

Scarf

44"
(112 cm)

9½ (10, 10½)"
(24, 25.5, 27 cm)

22 (23, 24)"
(56, 58.5, 61 cm)

Front
&
Back

1½"
(4 cm)

20½ (22½, 24½)"
(52, 57, 62 cm)

This project was knitted with 16 (17, 18) balls of Muench Yarns' *Lamour*, color #12, .88 oz (25 g) = approx. 87 yards (79.5 m) per ball.

La Dolce Vita
SILKY RIBBON KNIT

I T'S A "SWEET LIFE" WHEN YOU WORK WITH A SILKY, LIGHTWEIGHT RIBBON OF MICROFIBER AND NYLON AND A QUICK KNIT IN STOCKINETTE ON LARGE NEEDLES. THE FINISHED SWEATER IS SOFTLY STRETCHY BUT CONFORMS TO THE BODY AND ALWAYS KEEPS ITS SHAPE. A PERSONAL FAVORITE FOR ALL-SEASON WEAR, DAY OR NIGHT, AND IT TRAVELS ANYWHERE.

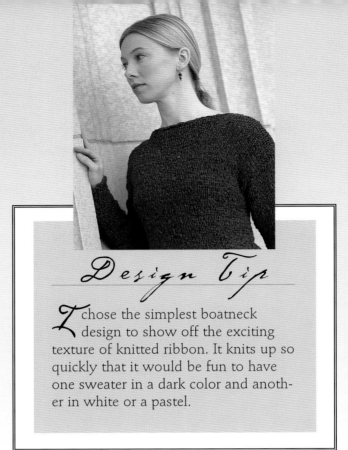

Sizes
Small (medium, large)

Finished Measurements
34 (36, 38) inches (86.5, 91.5, 96.5 cm)

Materials
792 (891, 990) yards (724, 814.5, 905.5 m) of 75% microfiber/25% nylon yarn, bulky weight.
Knitting needles in size 13 U.S. (9 mm)
Tapestry needle for sewing seams

Gauge
12 sts and 16 rows = 4 inches (10 cm)
Always take time to check your gauge.

Pattern Stitch
Stockinette
Row 1: Knit, right side.
Row 2: Purl, wrong side.

Back
Cast on 52 (54, 56) sts.
Work in stockinette to 21 (22, 23) inches (53.5, 56, 58.5 cm). Bind off.

Front
Work same as back.

Sleeves
Cast on 20 sts (same for all sizes).
Work in stockinette, increasing 1 st each side every 5th row, to 19 (19½, 20) inches (48.5, 49.5, 51 cm). Bind off.

Finishing
Sew shoulder seams, leaving a 10-inch neck opening.
Sew armhole, sleeve, and side seams.

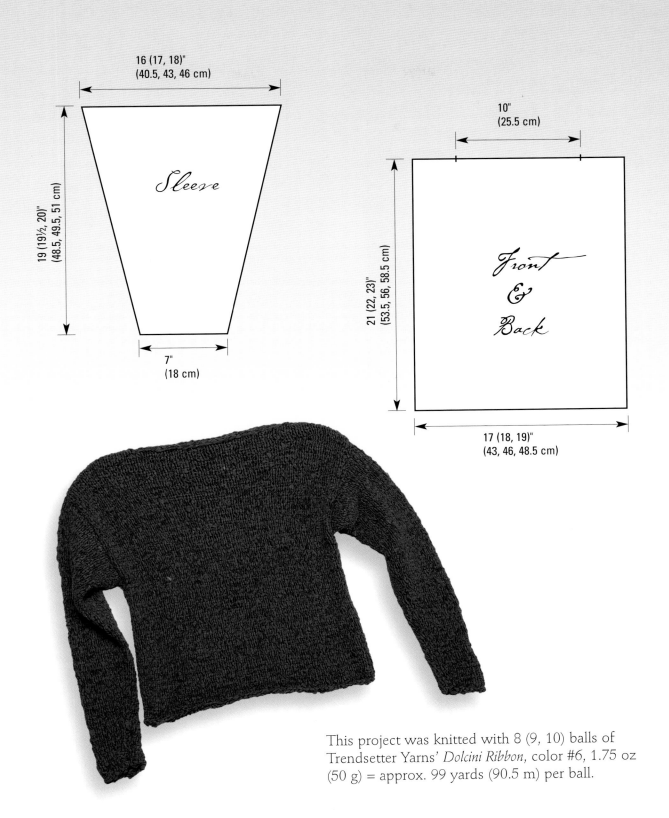

16 (17, 18)"
(40.5, 43, 46 cm)

Sleeve

19 (19½, 20)"
(48.5, 49.5, 51 cm)

7"
(18 cm)

10"
(25.5 cm)

Front
&
Back

21 (22, 23)"
(53.5, 56, 58.5 cm)

17 (18, 19)"
(43, 46, 48.5 cm)

This project was knitted with 8 (9, 10) balls of Trendsetter Yarns' *Dolcini Ribbon*, color #6, 1.75 oz (50 g) = approx. 99 yards (90.5 m) per ball.

Bamboo Stitch
V-NECK

EMPTY YOUR MIND FOR A WHILE AND FOCUS ON THE REPETITIVE MANTRA OF THE BAMBOO STITCH, A SIMPLE TWO-ROW PATTERN WITH AN INTRICATE-LOOKING RESULT. THE YARN IS A FINE MERINO/SILK COMBINATION AND THE STYLE IS A CLOSE FITTING V-NECK WITH MATCHING SCARF. THE COLOR IS A RICH ORCHID, BUT THE STITCH WOULD SHOW WELL IN ANY PASTEL, OR WHITE, IVORY, BEIGE—YOU CHOOSE!

119

Scarf

7"
(18 cm)

Design Tip

*E*ven though this is a small needle project, the pattern itself is much simpler than you would imagine. It's only a two-row pattern, with the main concentration on row 1, the second row being an all-purl row. After a few pattern repeats, you'll know the bamboo stitch by heart.

Sizes

Small (medium, large)

Finished Measurements

36 (38, 40) inches (91.5, 96.5, 101.5 cm)

Materials

Approx. 1800 (1980, 2160) yards (1646, 1810.5, 1975 m) of 75% extra-fine merino wool/25% silk yarn, sport weight
Knitting needles in size 6 U.S. (4 mm)
Crochet hook size E
Tapestry needle for sewing seams

Gauge

26 sts and 32 rows = 4 inches (10 cm)
Always take time to check your gauge.

Pattern Stitch

Bamboo stitch (over a multiple of 2 + 2 edge sts)
Row 1 (right side): K1 (edge st), *yo (wrap yarn over the right-hand needle), k2, pass the yo over the 2 knit sts*. Repeat from * to * ending with k1 (edge st).
Row 2: Purl.
Repeat rows 1 and 2.

Back

Cast on 118 (126, 132) sts.
Work in pattern until piece measures 20 (21, 22) inches (51, 53.5, 56 cm). Bind off.

Front

Work same as back to 13 (14, 15) inches (33, 35.5, 38 cm).
To shape neck: Work 59 (63, 66) sts. To split for V, join second ball of yarn and work to end. Working both sides at once, decrease 1 st at neck edges every other row to same length as back 20 (21, 22) inches (51, 53.5, 56 cm).
Bind off.

Sleeves

Cast on 52 (56, 60) sts.
Work in pattern, increasing 1 st each side every 6th row, until piece measures 19 (19½, 20) inches (48.5, 49.5, 51 cm).
Bind off.

Scarf

Cast on 46 stitches.
Work in pattern to 50 inches (127 cm).
Bind off.

Finishing

Sew shoulder, armhole, side, and sleeve seams.
The neckline requires the following finish: with right side facing and using crochet hook E, slip-stitch evenly into every other stitch. (Slip-stitch = insert hook into stitch; wrap the yarn over the hook from back to front; draw a loop through both the stitch and the loop on the hook.)

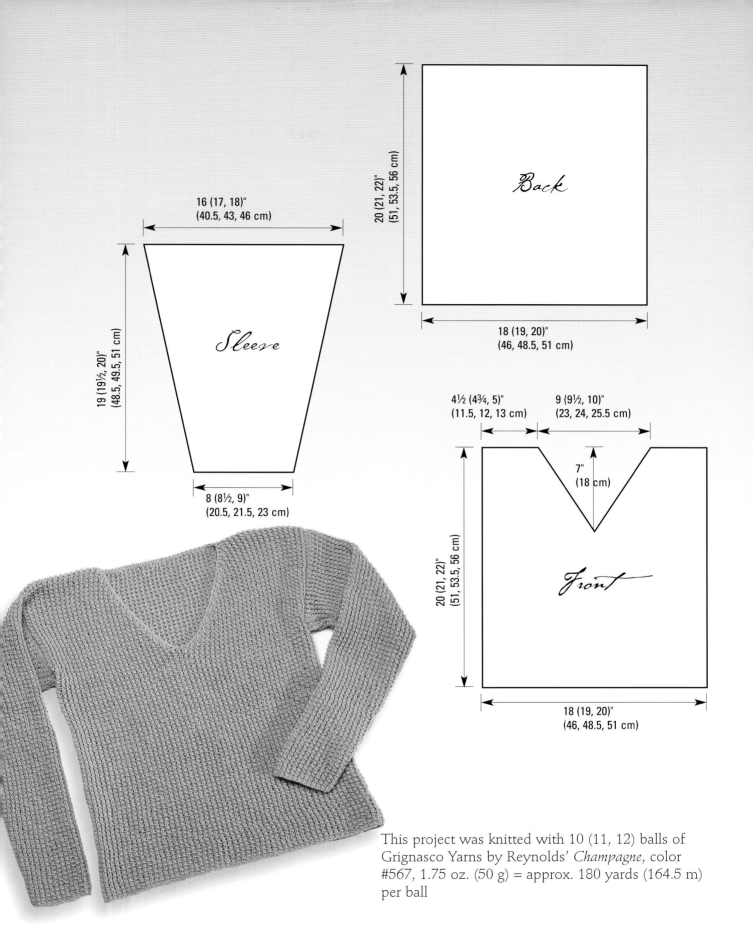

16 (17, 18)"
(40.5, 43, 46 cm)

Sleeve

19 (19½, 20)"
(48.5, 49.5, 51 cm)

8 (8½, 9)"
(20.5, 21.5, 23 cm)

Back

20 (21, 22)"
(51, 53.5, 56 cm)

18 (19, 20)"
(46, 48.5, 51 cm)

4½ (4¾, 5)"
(11.5, 12, 13 cm)

9 (9½, 10)"
(23, 24, 25.5 cm)

7"
(18 cm)

Front

20 (21, 22)"
(51, 53.5, 56 cm)

18 (19, 20)"
(46, 48.5, 51 cm)

This project was knitted with 10 (11, 12) balls of Grignasco Yarns by Reynolds' *Champagne*, color #567, 1.75 oz. (50 g) = approx. 180 yards (164.5 m) per ball

Lacy & LIGHT MOHAIR

THIS LACY, ALMOST WEB-LIKE, SILKY MOHAIR IS ONE OF MY MOST SUCCESSFUL EXPERIMENTS WITH THIN YARN ON LARGE NEEDLES. WORN OVER A CAMISOLE, THIS SWEATER IS LIGHT AS A FEATHER. WITH PLENTY OF EXTRA MATERIAL IN ITS ONE-SIZE-FITS ALL DESIGN, IT LOOKS BEST KNOTTED AT THE HIP FOR SHAPE.

Design Tip

*E*ven though this is an airy, lacy sweater, the mohair in the yarn keeps you surprisingly warm. The style is boxy, very wide, loose, and looks really elegant with a hip knot tied at the side. Black was my first choice for this design, but you might also consider bright scarlet or turquoise, as well as a pastel or neutral.

Sizes
One size fits all

Finished Measurements
48 inches (122 cm)

Materials
Approx. 864 yards (790 m) of 61% super kid mohair/8% wool/31% polyamide yarn, fingering weight
Knitting needles in size 9 U.S. (5.5 mm)
Tapestry needle for sewing seams

Gauge
22 sts and 20 rows = 4 inches (10 cm)
Always take time to check your gauge.

Pattern Stitch
Rib
Row 1: K1, p1. Repeat row 1.

Back
Cast on 138 sts.
Work pattern to 22 inches (56 cm). Bind off.

Front
Work same as back.

Sleeves
Cast on 52 sts.
Work pattern, increasing 1 st each side every 4th row, to 19½ inches (49.5 cm). Bind off.

Finishing
Sew shoulder seams, leaving a 12-inch (30.5 cm) neck opening.
Sew sleeve, side, and underarm seams.
Tie loose knot at hip.

6½"
(16.5 cm)

12"
(30.5 cm)

22"
(56 cm)

Front
&
Back

25"
(63.5 cm)

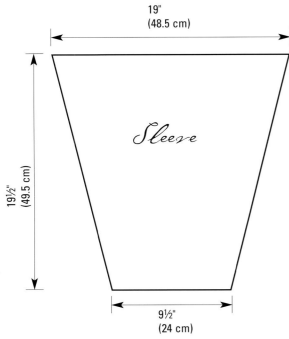

Sleeve

19"
(48.5 cm)

19½"
(49.5 cm)

9½"
(24 cm)

This project was knitted with 4 balls of Karabella Yarns' *Lace Mohair,* color #250, 1.75 oz (50 g) = approx. 216 yards (197.5 m) per ball.

Acknowledgments

Thank you from the bottom of my heart to all who helped make *Knitting Simple Sweaters from Luxurious Yarns* possible:

My very close friend and knitter, Jeannie Moran, who—with her superior knowledge of this art, her skills, and her patience—was able to decipher the hieroglyphics of my designs and produce exactly what I had in mind

My dear friends Kathy Diekmann and Anna Alessandria, both talented knitters and designers, for the fine work they accomplished

Kirsten Muench, of Muench Yarns, Inc., for asking me to design for her company and for encouraging me to write this book

The yarn companies that generously contributed their catalogs and yarns for me to use in many of the designs:

* Classic Elite
* JCA, distributors of Reynolds and Grignasco Yarns
* Muench Yarns
* Trendsetter Yarns

My hard-working editor, Marcianne Miller, who kept me focused with her knowledge and wit; Senior Editor Deborah Morgenthal, who gently took me through the initial stages of this long-range project; and Nicole Tuggle, Executive Assistant to the Publishing Director, who rooted for me right from the beginning

The consummate artists who made this book a visual feast, Dana M. Irwin, art director, and Sandra Stambaugh, photographer

The models who enhanced my designs with their serenity and natural beauty, including especially my daughter, Lisa, for her graceful and elegant poses on the front cover and within the book

Millinery designers Barbara Zaretsky (pages 32, 36 and 122) and Marlene Miller (page 44)

Those who provided the spectacular shooting locations:

* Aaron Zaretsky and Ann McMartin of the Grove Arcade Public Market in Asheville, NC, 828-252-7799 (www.grovearcade.com)

* Judy Carter and Susan Sluyter of the Wintersun Inn in Fairview, NC, 828-628-7890 (www.innatwintersun.com)

A NOTE ABOUT SUPPLIERS

Usually, the supplies you need for making the projects in Lark knitting books can be found at your local yarn supply store. Occasionally, however, you may need to buy materials or tools from specialty suppliers. In order to provide you with the most up-to-date information, we have created suppliers listings on our website, which we update on a regular basis. Visit us at www.larkbooks.com, click on "Craft Supply Sources," then click on the name of the book or the topic "Knitting" on the "Book Categories" list. You'll find numerous companies listed with their web address and/or mailing address and phone number.

Three special friends and knitters have been working with me for about 20 years: Jeannie Moran has her own sweater design and knitting business; Anna Alessandria, a pharmacologist, and Kathy Diekmann, a psychologist, are also knitwear designers.

THE MODELS

Left to right, top row: Lisa Renee Cohen, Mary E. Dunning, Victoria Nordstrom Fall; middle row: Kimberly Sue Luke, Amber Lauren Martz-Johnson , Meredith Ann McCusker; bottom row: Cayanne Bead Ramuten, Juliet S. Werner

A
Angora/nylon blend yarn, 33
Angora/wool yarn, 111

B
Ballet neck style, 25
Bamboo stitch, 119
Boatneck style, 33, 49, 67, 74, 75, 84, 87, 111, 114

C
Cashmere yarn, 90
Cotton/acrylic blend, 49
Cotton/linen blend, 25
Cotton/viscose/polyester blend, 21
Cotton yarn, 78
Crewneck style, 17

D
Dropped shoulders, 12

E
Eyelet rib stitch, 75, 111

F
Funnel neck style, 37, 61, 71, 103

G
Garter stitch, 38, 90
Gauge, 11-12

H
Hooded pullover, 90

K
Kid mohair, 17, 41, 45

L
Large-needle projects, 33, 45, 49, 53, 61, 71, 84, 103, 114, 123
Lattice cables, 74
Luxury yarn knitting tips, 11-13

M
Merino/microfiber blend, 81
Merino/nylon/wool ribbon, 84
Merino/silk blend, 94, 119
Merino/wool yarn, 57
Microfiber, 103
Mohair/wool/nylon blend, 17, 41, 45, 53, 87, 123

N
Nylon ribbon yarn, 29, 41, 67, 114

P
Polyester ribbon, 99
Pure new wool, 61

R
Rayon/cotton/linen blend, 107
Rib stitch, 94

S
Scarf projects, 81, 111, 119
Scoop neck style, 29
Sequined yarn, 87
Shoulder seam, 12
Silk yarn, 17, 94, 119
Sleeveless turtleneck style, 21
Sleeveless style, 37, 84, 87, 99
Slip-stitch rib, 61
Split-scoop neck style, 107
Stockinette stitch, 17, 21, 29, 33, 37, 41, 45, 49, 57, 71, 81, 84, 98, 103, 107, 114

T
Turtleneck style, 45, 57, 94
Tweed, 17
Twisted rib, 57

V
Viscose microfiber/wool yarn, 37
V-neck style, 41, 119

W
Whip stitch, 12
Wool/rayon yarn, 71